The Power Experiment

-=!=-

An Original Sex-Fantasy Engineering Project and a Philosophy of Heterosexual Interaction

Designed By

-=!=-

The Rock Hard Dinosaur Killer

-=!=-

[NOT RECOMENDED FOR MINORS]

authorHOUSE®

AuthorHouse™ UK
1663 Liberty Drive
Bloomington, IN 47403 USA
www.authorhouse.co.uk
Phone: 0800.197.4150

Published by AuthorHouse 03/12/2018

ISBN: 978-1-5462-8337-9 (sc)
ISBN: 978-1-5462-8336-2 (e)

Library of Congress Control Number: 2018902697

Print information available on the last page.

This book is printed on acid-free paper.

Legal Information

All names and characters portrayed in this book are fictional. The events in this book may not have happened!

This document is a textual expression of the design of "The Sex-Lovers Fantasy Mind-Driver System", to which design rights apply.

This document is a copy of an electronic database containing "The Sex-Lovers Fantasy Mind-Driver System" symbols, characters, concepts, resources and methods, which has database rights accordingly.

The pseudonym of "The Rock Hard Dinosaur Killer"© and the book titles *"The Power Experiment"*© and *"A Bold Birthday Surprise"*© are copyrighted by the author, Mr Stephen A. Dimery, BSc, in the year 2018.

The

Sex-Lovers

Fantasy

Mind-Driver System

-=!=-

This pleasure-craft system is designed for

heterosexual human interaction,

using sexual information as mind drivers

within the species 'Human',

for the purposes of generating pleasure.

-=!=-

All Definitions Are Local
to This Book

sex. v. A method of human interaction.

lover. n. A person who enjoys the giving, receiving, and practicing of concepts, methods, and resources that are involved in love-making rituals, for the purpose of putting pleasure in the world.

fantasy. n. An elaborate or far-fetched, imaginary literary creation, unrestricted by reality.

mind-driver. n. An idea that activates the mind.

system. n. A set of parts assembled into a complete whole, usually for a purpose.

heterosexual. n. A person who is sexually attracted to the opposite gender.

power. n. An ability to affect, that is available for use.

philosophy. n. A term for this belief system concept involving ideas and beliefs, such as the value of joy as an experience, the value of personal relationships, social behavior, ritualism, emotional reactions, and the right of personal happiness.

experiment. v. A scientific procedure to find out or prove something, without a predefined result.

Contents

A short introduction to the "The Power Experiment".

-=!=-

This introduces the subject of belief systems. Rather than expose all the belief systems that I have studied, I intend to create a new one with some of the good beliefs that I have encountered, called "The Positive Vital Entity Belief System".

-=!=-

This team is the foundation of the new constructed belief system. Although we experience some form of difficulty with our lives, all of us are prepared to experiment with each others' good ideas to learn a better way of thinking.

-=!=-

The resources that we intend to use are fantasy ideas and beliefs which may at first appear to be alien to our natural selves. It is important to note that it is possible to adopt these beliefs for pleasure, and that the use of them within a physical environment may not be practical.

-=!=-

Once a resource is applied with intent to a purpose, it becomes a tool. Tools may be assembled in any order or configuration to provide a working prototype of a solution.

-=!=-

This is a list of solutions that have been successful in the production of mutual pleasure (which is the team's common purpose) during human interaction between team members.

-=!=-

Fun literature so that you get the point of the book, which is to have a laugh with your sexual partners.

-=!=-

This section discusses a couple of component belief systems of the "Positive Vital Entity Belief System".

-=!=-

Information derived from the perceptions of the team members' experience with "Positive Vital Entity Belief System" whilst using the "The Sex-Lovers Fantasy Mind-Driver System".

-=!=-

A free competition. For you to express bravado!

-=!=-

Preface

Human interaction is a phenomenon that occurs as part of the natural ability of humans to learn intelligently. A human can interact with an entity in order to learn about it.

Whilst interacting, the five major physical senses supply information to the brain, and the brain is the location where all information is calculated to form an understanding of the environment. Other senses may include your sense of balance or maybe even common sense and intuition.

Sight – You can see boats on the horizon.
Sound – You can hear a wave on the beach.
Touch – You can feel a currency note.
Smell – You can detect that which is scent.
Taste – You can taste your food.

Sexual activity is social behavior. Therefore all sexual activity requires the voluntary participation of more than one person. In the case of a sexual idea, we use personality driven fantasy construction to place enjoyable concepts in each others minds.

-=!=-

Warning: Ideas are the origin of our behavior.

Because this system can affect the desires and behaviors of a person, it is suggested that time is designated for the purpose of producing pleasure within a relationship, via a time tabling method, to maintain a sensible approach to the subject.

Such a time table may be as simple as using every Saturday evening to do one fantasy per month. This would allow a couple or group of people to spend one evening per week on each of the following activities: preparing, experimenting, practicing, and fulfilling a fantasy. If so, it might be possible to use thirty-six fantasies over three years and have been selective enough to have discarded twenty-four.

Bear in mind that some of these fantasies are exactly that: a behavior which could not be fulfilled safely or to the satisfaction of all parties involved. Some of them sound exciting but may not be practical. An example of this could be when it is suggested that an instrument is used with maximum force, but common sense would dictate light application.

It is the duty of all those who take part to ensure good communication and agreement before and during a fantasy. If anyone uses the command words "no" or "stop", then all parties should comply.

These fantasies are not designed to inflict power over another person. This system is designed for people in relationships who rely on trust and good intention. All relationships are considered to be one-to-one, even within a group. An example of this might be a married couple or even a threesome, in which there are six points of view on three relationships.

-=!=-

Introduction

This section introduces the subject of belief systems. I have studied the beliefs of many other people during my lifetime as a hobby, on the understanding that people's beliefs affect their understanding of life and their behavior, as well as their ability to be happy.

The method by which we are going to practice and understand the power of beliefs on the human mind is to experiment with apparently random or fictional information and build what is called a belief machine.

We are going to start with a working definition of a belief machine: a short story that we can pretend is true, in order to find out if we enjoy believing it! The reason that we adopt this attitude towards that which is supposed to be a scientific experiment is so that we can throw out any ideas that are potentially upsetting before they cause a problem.

For the duration of this experiment, the belief machines that we are going to use will be concerned with sexual fantasies. This is because we assume that all people will have at least a desire to experience sex in some form or other, and that these fantasies are a safe method of experimentation with an activity with which we would all like to claim competence. In other words, whether you read this book because you think you are good in bed and want to prove you understand the content, or whether you read this book to understand what sex is all about, you will get some good ideas about how to use a professionally constructed mind-driver system that you can share with your friends and lovers.

-=!=-

In order to establish whether this experiment has had any effect on your belief system, try answering some of these questions before and after you have read the book, comparing your two sets of answers.

-=!=-

How aware are you of your current lovemaking system?									
0	1	2	3	4	5	6	7	8	9

How aware are you of your partner's lovemaking system?									
0	1	2	3	4	5	6	7	8	9

How aware are you of your current dominant qualities?									
0	1	2	3	4	5	6	7	8	9

How aware are you of your current submissive qualities?									
0	1	2	3	4	5	6	7	8	9

How much of your bedroom interaction practices are sexual or loving?								
Sex	All	Most	Some	One answer either side	Some	Most	All	Love

How good are you at sex?									
0	1	2	3	4	5	6	7	8	9

How good are you at love?									
0	1	2	3	4	5	6	7	8	9

How much sexual power do you have?									
0	1	2	3	4	5	6	7	8	9

How many sex styles are you aware of?									
0	1	2	3	4	5	6	7	8	9

How many lovemaking styles are you aware of?									
0	1	2	3	4	5	6	7	8	9

How kinky are you?									
0	1	2	3	4	5	6	7	8	9

Are you confident that you are good in bed?									
0	1	2	3	4	5	6	7	8	9

-=!=-

The Sex Deity Club

Resident Male Sex Deity [Master]

Num	Tag	Character	Understanding	Favorite Concepts	Favorite Fantasy	Tools
XX	Rock Hard Dinosaur Killer	???	Life Partner	Love	Sex Maniacs Kiss	Power

Resident Female Sex Deities [Divas]

Num	Tag	Character	Understanding	Favorite Concepts	Favorite Fantasy	Tools
01	Devils Decoy	Dom	Life Partner	Power	Kink Trip	Love
02	Fem Fatal	Sub	Life Partner	Power	Blokey Banter	Respect
03	Fetish Fiance	Dom	Life Partner	Power	Porn Star	Loyalty
04	Generous Genius	Sub	Life Partner	Power	Girl Power	Honor
05	Know Limits	Dom	Life Partner	Power	Slut Shag	Prowess
06	Mischievous Model	Sub	Life Partner	Power	Yo-Yo Gym Dancer	Joy
07	Outrageous Spirit	Sub	Life Partner	Power	Nursey Treatment	Honesty
08	Rainbow Dancer	Sub	Life Partner	Power	Wank Bitch	Pleasure
09	Reckless Ruin	Dom	Life Partner	Power	Love and Beauty	Innocence
10	Working Girl	Sub	Life Partner	Power	Dragon's Kiss	Art

-=!=-

-=!=-

Party Guest Females List

Num	Tag	Character	Understanding	Uniform	Concept	Main Tools
11	Bashful Bride	Dom	Life Partner	Static Rainbow	Purity	Love
12	Big Hair	Dom	Playmate	Sex Slut Uniform	Dominatrix	Cotton Lash
13	Brave Bitch	Sub	Lover	Stockings and Heels	Ascendency	Latex
14	Cock Rider	Sub	Life Partner	Maids Outfit	Inspiration	Heels
15	Curvaceous Courtesan	Dom	Lover	Nurses Uniform	Sex Technician	Pornography
16	Delicate Diva	Sub/Dom	Life Partner	Thigh Boots	Joy	Virtue
17	Delightful Dame	Sub/Dom	Playmate	Naked	God	Life Force Energy
18	Descent Damsel	Sub	Playmate	Leather	sp*nk Slut	Lightweight Crop
19	Fickle Flirt	Sub/Dom	Life Partner	Sex Slut Uniform	Desire	Silk Gloves
20	Freaky Floozy	Sub	Playmate	Silk and Satin	E=MC2	Ballet
21	Flirtatious Tart	Sub	Playmate	Naked	Oral Worship	Kindness
22	Gifted Girlie	Sub	Life Partner	Liquid Rainbow	Ritualism	Fetish
23	Glamorous Granny	Sub	Playmate	Silk and Satin	Purity	Kissing
24	Gleeful Gloater	Sub	Playmate	Silk and Satin	Kink	Beauty
25	High Fidelity	Sub	Life Partner	Lipstick	Romance	Shagging

26	Holy Moly	Dom	Playmate	Sex Slut Uniform	God	Power
27	Honest Individual	Sub	Playmate	Silk and Satin	Submission	Stiletto Shoes
28	Horny Hooker	Dom	Life Partner	Sex Slut Uniform	Money	Tits
29	Insane Bitch	Dom	Playmate	Naked	Erotica	Attitude
30	Iron Maiden	Dom	Life Partner	Static Rainbow	Discipline	Crop
31	Killer Shag	Sub	Playmate	Sex Slut Uniform	Pleasure	Kisses
32	Kinky Kernel	Dom	Playmate	Sex Slut Uniform	Obsession	Kink
33	Lady Lore	Sub	Playmate	Leather and Lace	Friendship	Trust
34	Lick-able Lover	Dom	Life Partner	Leather and Lace	Correction	Riding Crop
35	Loyalty Prize	Sub	Playmate	Leather and Lace	Slut Techniques	Rubber
36	Luxury Lady	Dom	Playmate	Sex Slut Uniform	Control	Feathers
37	Mad Mistress	Sub/Dom	Life Partner	Stockings and Heels	Persistence	Peephole Bra
38	Man Eater	Dom	Playmate	Leather & Lace	Extrovert	Beauty
39	Medieval Menace	Sub	Playmate	Leather & Lace	Flight	Feathers
40	Mi Passion	Sub	Playmate	Silky Stockings	Uniforms	Positive Emotions
41	Mrs Christmas	Sub	Playmate	Red Play-Suit	Fun	Laughter
42	VIP	Sub/Dom	Playmate	Naked	Telepathy	Orgasmic Stimulation

-=!=-

Stereotype Character Classification	Qualities
Professional Female	Egalitarian in principle, this woman is proud of the number and quality of the sex tricks that she can perform.
Sp*nk Bitch	Dominant all the time, this woman drives men hard to get their sp*nk out.
Rubber Slut	Egalitarian in principle, this woman doesn't mind being on top or underneath. She loves to be shagged by her man while she is in her favorite black sheen rubber catsuit.
Girly-as-Shag	Submissive all the time, this woman enjoys exciting her man by wearing soft-textured lingerie and screaming, "Give it to me, Sugar Daddy. I want your sp*nk!" when he shags her.
Wifey Slut	Egalitarian in principle, this woman's main concern is that she has taught pleasure to her man and that he feels cared for after he has been vulnerable. It is her aim to show him true love.
Bisexual Tart	Egalitarian in principle, this woman loves to have her lesbian fantasies knocked out of her head by her man's cock.
Submissive Slut	Submissive to women and dominant to men, will have a go at anything she's told to and loves sex.
Porn Star	Submissive to everyone, this woman loves the camera and enjoys to perform like an extrovert.
Visual Goddess	Perfect glamor model image and confidence in her beauty.
Love Robot	Submissive to sexual pleasure and loving emotion, this woman is a joy to share company with.
Brain Box	This woman pleases her man's mind and stimulates his body whilst developing his awareness of pleasure.
Domination Diva	Dominant in principle, this woman uses power and control techniques safely. She rewards her partner with blow-jobs when he responds to her commands.

-=!=-

Example Profile

Name: Rock Hard Dinosaur Killer

Sexuality: Heterosexual Male

Style: Big Hard Softy

Image Type/Class: Military

Motivation: Joy, Pleasure, and Rapture

Ambition: To have an orgasm that would kill a normal man

Goal: The achievement of perfection by personal definition

Ideal Vocation: Lipstick lesbian straightener

Best Previous Experience: The awe of perceiving female idols

Signature Sexual Gift: Prancing Unicorn

Favorite Phrase: "Get your pussy out! Uggg!"

Authorized Innovator For: Sex Engineering Research

Voice Type: Masculine Resonant

Example Profile

Name: Mental Harmony

Sexuality: Heterosexual Female Sub/Dom

Style: Maid

Image Type/Class: Sex Toy

Motivation: Marriage

Ambition: To convert her life partner into a spouse

Goal: The achievement of perfection by personal definition

Ideal Vocation: To be the lover of a "Wall of Death" rider

Best Previous Experience: The invention of "Pressure Sex"

Signature Sexual Gift: Cradle of the Stork

Favorite Phrase: "I know you only love me cos I've got a pussy!"

Authorized Innovator For: Nipple Fetishes

Voice Type: Feminine Saucy

Example Profile

Name: Mi Love

Sexuality: Heterosexual Female Submissive

Style: sp*nk Bitch

Image Type/Class: Nymphet

Motivation: Best Slut

Ambition: To give the first blow-job in space

Goal: The achievement of perfection by personal definition

Ideal Vocation: To be the queen of a small country

Best Previous Experience: The memory of her first threesome

Signature Sexual Gift: Wiggling Tiger-fish

Favorite Phrase: "I'm gonna wire you up so you can't stop squirting!"

Authorized Innovator For: Whip Fetishes

Voice Type: Feminine Happy

Example Profile

Name: Perfectly Maid

Sexuality: Heterosexual Female Submissive

Style: Sugar and Spice

Image Type/Class: Nymphet

Motivation: Young Love

Ambition: To excite Sugar Daddy until he squirts his love all over her

Goal: The achievement of perfection by personal definition

Ideal Vocation: To be the lover of a drag car racer

Best Previous Experience: The gift of a rainbow catsuit

Signature Sexual Gift: Extravagant Crab

Favorite Phrase: "I need you to empty yourself in my pussy!"

Authorized Innovator For: Glove Fetishes

Voice Type: Feminine Spicy

Example Profile

Name: Police Honey Trap

Sexuality: Heterosexual Female Submissive

Style: Naughty Nurse

Image Type/Class: Aphrodite

Motivation: Perfection

Ambition: To experience the ultimate heterosexual activity

Goal: The achievement of perfection by personal definition

Ideal Vocation: To be the world's best rubber fetish model

Best Previous Experience: To have given herself completely to her husband

Signature Sexual Gift: Divine Butterfly Stance

Favorite Phrase: "Lick it and worship my pussy!"

Authorized Innovator For: Latex Fetishes

Voice Type: Feminine Squeaky

Example Profile

Name: Randy Ruthless

Sexuality: Heterosexual Female Dominant

Style: Dominatrix

Image Type/Class: Spouse

Motivation: True Friendship

Ambition: To perform the Dance of the Seven Veils

Goal: The achievement of perfection by personal definition

Ideal Vocation: To use a telepathically delivered orgasm device

Best Previous Experience: The invention of the short-tailed energy lash

Signature Sexual Gift: Splaying Peacock

Favorite Phrase: "I'm gonna sit on you with my pussy!"

Authorized Innovator For: C*ck Fetishes

Voice Type: Feminine Husky

Example Profile

Name: Virgin Virago

Sexuality: Heterosexual Female Sub/Dom

Style: Chamber Maid

Image Type/Class: Aphrodite

Motivation: Nostalgia

Ambition: To be recognized as stunningly beautiful

Goal: The achievement of perfection by personal definition

Ideal Vocation: To be the lover of an astronaut

Best Previous Experience: The invention of the Power Flash

Signature Sexual Gift: Sacred Swan Stance

Favorite Phrase: "I love wanking you off!"

Authorized Innovator For: Basque Fetishes

Voice Type: Feminine Creamy

Example Profile

Name: Willful Wench

Sexuality: Heterosexual Female Dominant

Style: Blow-job Secretary

Image Type/Class: Spouse

Motivation: Best Slut

Ambition: To control her spouse until he orgasms on demand

Goal: The achievement of perfection by personal definition

Ideal Vocation: To be the lover of an Olympic gold medalist

Best Previous Experience: Her "Sex Goddess" award

Signature Sexual Gift: Kinky Hummingbird

Favorite Phrase: "For that, I'm gonna to staple your nose to my pussy!"

Authorized Innovator For: Pussy Fetishes

Voice Type: Feminine Chocolaty

Resources

The reason that this sex fantasy engineering system is supposed to work is because it is designed on the principle that the human brain responds to the information delivered to it. The specific response that we are looking for is an emotion called pleasure. Unfortunately, owing to the fact that we each have learned a different belief system, we cannot guarantee that what we find pleasurable to think about will be acceptable to another person. In order to give you an example of what I am talking about, we will use the statement, "Granny ate all the cheese!"

In this example, some children are in a classroom, and they overhear the teacher say to another adult, "Granny ate all the cheese!" Initially, some of the class will dismiss this statement as nothing to do with them.

They understand that they are not involved in this conversation.

Their grandmother is deceased.

They are uninterested and couldn't care less.

Of the children who respond to this piece of information, there will be different responses for different reasons. Some will understand that the mentioned grandmother is not related to them, and will ignore the information. This is a deliberate response.

Some may consider that if the statement was concerned with their own grandmother, then they are sad because they will go hungry on account of not having a cheese sandwich available.

Some may consider that if the statement was concerned with their own grandmother, then they are happy because their grandmother is no longer hungry.

The point of the above example is to illustrate that if you intend to interact with your partner, then you are both better off when you have taken the time to learn a bit about each others belief system and personality. A useful phrase that applies to this situation is this, "The personality drives the machine." If you don't know somebody well enough, you can get an unexpected response to the information you give them.

In order to build a Sex-Lovers belief machine with a desired partner, it is therefore necessary to make sure that she understands your intention and that you have her permission. This requires voluntary communication and confirmation of understanding. The possible concern for error in what we are trying to achieve is that either of the two parties in the relationship could make an assumption that the partner has understood something without it being true. The obvious and only way forward on this subject is to be honest and accurate about your beliefs, responses, and feelings. The benefit of this approach is to guarantee that there will be an opportunity to settle any misunderstandings or false assumptions. This will help us achieve a mutual and agreeable understanding of our partners.

Our best resource is to have the good intent of issuing pleasure towards our partner free of charge, which is often understood by them intuitively but should be confirmed. This intent should be mutual, as should the joint understanding of what you are trying to do with the relationship. In order to intelligently design what you both want to achieve, a recommended method is to identify your common beliefs and goals to use them as tools, or building blocks, for the construction of your mutual belief machine.

While you learn to exchange these common thoughts for the purposes of pleasure, you will benefit each other as you come to associate pleasure with the personality of your partner. The purpose of the system is to allow you to learn about your partner as a person, using sexual fantasies as a medium. The goal of the system, and the individuals in it, should be to understand happiness within the jointly owned relationships. If you consider that you are the owner of your half of the relationship, instead of owning the person on the other end of it, it is probable that you will both learn the relationship is worth having. In this system, we generate loving relationships using fun and play.

Tools and Techniques

There are various mental tools and idea systems employed in the Sex-Lovers Fantasy Mind-Driver System. The simplest tool is the belief machine, and there are others ranging in complexity that form the basis of various life systems.

The tools called belief machines are a set of coherently assembled ideas that form a working concept in the mind. This principle is the basis of the mind-driver system. In this case, each belief machine is designed to elicit a response of pleasure with a sexually arousing fantasy that is appealing to the loving partners.

Example Belief Machine

A core instinctive response is generated in the mind of a heterosexual person upon the perception of an attractive potential mating partner. It does not matter whether I perceive my lover via sight, sound, touch, taste, smell, memory, or sixth sense. The perception of their identity generates a positive, conscious effect that has been learned through repetitive recognition and pleasure on contact. The development of this emotional mental reaction has occurred over time, during the course of our relationship. Through the course of our social interaction experiences, I have taken pleasure in my lover's existence, and this is instinctively reinforced each time we meet. I have learned that they are my lover, and I am happy.

-=!=-

-=!=-

A Concept Definition of Engineering as a Mental Tool

This text explains what engineering is and how to use it. Let us first see a few definitions of the word.

Definition: the application of science to designing things

Explanation: the application of science in the design, planning, construction, and maintenance of buildings, machines, and other manufactured things

Definition: a profession involving technical designing

Explanation: a branch of engineering pursued as a profession, such as civil engineering or electronic engineering

Example: Software Engineer: A person who is capable of designing, constructing, testing, and maintaining a software component or component-based system. A software system is normally dedicated to a purpose and designed to provide that purpose as a service.

Definition: contrivance

Explanation: the planning or bringing about of something, especially when done with ingenuity or secretiveness.

With these definitions (which were taken from the dictionary within the word processing program Microsoft Word), it might be sensible to establish one definition that is built up and makes sense to all three. I feel this is necessary because I believe that a word represents an idea. There are ninety-six words within the three definitions provided, and so I suggest that these definitions are actually ways in which the word *engineering* can be defined or used from different perspectives. First, I have selected the most important words from all three explanations and given a short definition of each, in an attempt to let you know how I intend to use each of them in the new definition.

Application: the use something is put to, or the process of putting it to use

Science: the method of confirming information using recorded and repeatable experiments, which give predictable results

Designing: generating thoughts, usually for a purpose

Profession: an occupation that requires extensive education or specialized training

Technical: specific details normally concerned with a defined subject or trade

Planning: working out in advance how something is to be done or organized

Maintenance: work that is done to upkeep or repair something

Ingenuity: cleverness and originality

Capable: possessing the qualities needed to do a particular thing

Person: an individual human being

Secretiveness: unwillingness to divulge information

Constructing: building something

Testing: challenging someone or something for purposes of proof of validity

Component: a part of something, usually of something bigger

System: a combination of related parts organized into a complex whole

Purpose: the goal or intended outcome of something

Service: the use that can be had from a machine or piece of equipment

If you were to try to make one sentence with these words in their current order, you may arrive at a statement that is not a fluent construction of English. This may not represent an accurate description of the definition of the word *engineering*. By understanding the concepts behind each of the words in the list, it should be possible to generate a theory that enforces the understanding behind the word *engineering*. In order to create a logical and fully functional theory, it would be reasonable to combine the words into sentences that are grammatically correct. After I have produced the new definition, I will give some explanatory notes that may explain some points.

Engineering

New Definition: A specific type of thinking process, used by a professional person who has the capability of applying knowledge to a specific purpose. In order to gain qualification and experience, engineers must acquire and maintain various types of technical information, which should preferably be scientifically proven and considered a resource. Allowing for the practice that each idea they possess is considered a component, they should construct solution systems with designing and planning methods. Ingenious solutions will not fail any method of testing. A successful solution may be repeatedly used to service any instance of the original purpose for which it was designed. Resources, methods, and previous successful solutions will accumulate into a toolset over time. Sensitive information may be justified as a trade secret on the grounds that it may inflict damage on the self, others, or the environment if used incorrectly.

Notes

The new definition was engineered using the English language.

It would be possible to consider the above definition as the combined knowledge of four different people. The original three definitions could be supplied by three separate individuals who have tried to explain, with one word or phrase, what understanding or meaning they have of the word *engineering*.

In each case, the explanation represents the experience gained in the learning process of how to define the word.

The example given in definition two, however, was supplied to students who intended to become engineers before they started. It was supplied to the students by a professional teacher who understood that the chosen subject could be used as a learning vehicle. The phrase *learning vehicle* could be applied to any theoretical subject or practical experience, just by thinking about it.

Conscious thought is actually a brain operation method, and the whole brain is available as a resource, including the id.

-=!=-

A Concept Definition of Sexuality as a Mental Tool

A concept can be defined as a theory composed of a set of ideas or beliefs. In the case of sexuality, there are three main options to choose from: heterosexuality, homosexuality, and bisexuality.

Before we examine the options in any depth, let us first understand the fact that the reason these options exist is because in a society where the government supports freedom of choice, it will allow us to achieve self-definition by giving us that choice. In a population that believes they have the right to choose, all the time that you do not inflict harm on another person, your freedom of choice will remain intact, and you will have not committed a crime.

If there truly was only one possible answer, a self-respecting government would make the choice for you and enforce a law that governed the correct sexuality of the population.

In many cases, if you ask a person who is not of the same sexuality as yourself, "Why did you choose to be the sexuality that you claim to be?" their answer might be, "Because I had the choice!" Often they will support this answer with the defensive comment, "Just because I chose differently to you, it does not mean I am wrong!" From the perspective of the law, their argument is correct. You yourself are also entitled to use this argument to defend the choice that you made.

The obvious question here is to ask why there are different choices, when in a perfect world there would be an intelligent population that would examine every part of the subject and would therefore logically reach total agreement throughout, with everyone arriving at the same choice.

The correct perspective to take on this question may sound quite complicated but is actually simple. "We are animals that shag with ideas in our heads!" Although the phrase could be used as a catchphrase or a punchline, it is actually an acutely accurate statement. Given that ideas are the origin of our behavior, it is true that your choice of sexuality will be dependent on various factors and affect the way you behave.

There are many reasons to believe that a piece of information may be a worthy factor when choosing your sexuality. Here is a list of some of the factors that you may consider.

Do I want to have sex because I need to breed?

Do I want to have sex because I desire pleasure?

Am I sexually attracted to the opposite gender?

Am I sexually attracted to the same gender?

Am I confident that I am sexually attractive?

With which sexuality has the majority
of my friends identified?

Do I choose to be unique by comparative values?

Will my family, friends, or associates
be offended by my choice?

Am I right to believe that this is the correct choice?

Am I happy with the choice I have made?

Am I shagging people whom I like?

Do the people I shag like me?

Are there any other factors?

Having considered the legal environment and some factors that could influence your decision, let us consider the choices that you can make. In order to keep things simple, the three main sexualities of heterosexuality, homosexuality, and bisexuality have been suggested as the only three available. This is not strictly true. There are, for example, such options as celibacy, and asexuality.

Now that we have considered the legal aspects or requirement of the decision and the information needed to achieve one of the available options, it should have become apparent that the following situation is true: No matter which choice you make, there will always be an opportunity for someone to accuse you of being wrong for having made your selection of sexuality, purely because there are many options and the right to choose.

In my opinion, there is one obvious and best way to handle this potential problem when it occurs. Understand that when you have chosen your selection, it is correct for you. After you have understood this to be true, you will be able to justify your decision any way you like. However, I recommend that you only use scientific facts in your argument.

Here are only a few justifications for defending the choice of heterosexuality.

<u>It is my belief that there is only one type of sexuality.</u>

1. Because everybody is born of heterosexual activity, this must be our first option, because the concept is common to all of us. It is our first option and held by the majority of the population, and so everything else must be considered a minority group activity.

-=!=-

2. The definition of heterosexual activity is "to insert a penis into a vagina". This definition is called "true sex" or *f*cking*, and it can be performed for the following reasons:

   a. for pleasure

   b. for breeding

   c. a and b together.

-=!=-

3. This definition of *f*cking* is so accurate because both parties in the couple are applying their genitals to the activity in the correct manor. Consequently, it is the only accurate definition of heterosexual behavior. Therefore, the only heterosexual activity is to fuck, and everything else is to be considered as kink.

-=!=-

4. With this established fact in mind, it becomes apparent to the educated that there are many uneducated people on the planet who enjoy using the word *f*ck* but don't have a clue what they are talking about.
For example:

a. Homosexual men cannot *f*ck* each other, on the grounds that the technical definition of fucking requires a vagina.

b. Because men cannot engage sexually for the purpose of breeding and cannot actually *f*ck* each other on a technical level, there must be some definition of what gay men actually do to each other.

c. It is logical to assume that because only one of the males is actively sexual and the other is passive or submissive, then one of them is actually masturbating into or onto the other, and the other is experiencing kink.

d. It would be unfair not to observe that the active partner is technically capable of masturbation without the use of his hands, which can be applauded as a clever or sneaky trick.

e. Homosexual women cannot *f*ck* each other, on the grounds that the technical definition of fucking requires a penis.

f. Because women cannot engage sexually for the purpose of breeding and cannot actually *f*ck* each other on a technical level, there must be some definition of what gay women actually do to each other.

g. It is logical to assume that because women are designed to be penetrated, then it will affect their psychology, compared to a man. If you adopt the classic or traditional style of relationship, where the male penetrates and the female accepts, then it is easy to believe that men should be dominant and women should be submissive.

h. When considering lesbian activity in a couple, it is reasonable to assume that one of the partners must take an assertive or dominant role in order for either of them to achieve physical contact.

i. Therefore it can be concluded that these women are actually engaging in power games that happen to involve foreplay and oral worship, but it is nice to watch.

j. The end result of the conclusions from the above observations can only be that "Gay is kink", "Kink is not true sex", and "Homosexuality does not exist". If homosexuality does not exist, neither can bisexuality. Therefore the definition of homosexuality seems to be "people who distort true sex to create kink".

k. Having dealt with what are considered the main three options for the choice of sexuality, here's a word to the wise. There are many combinations of the sexuality concept in the mind, combined with physical behavior of the body and emotional satisfaction in the spirit. This allows for such phenomena as, for example the choice of a male lesbian. It is only when your personal combination matches the desires of a selected partner that you can achieve happiness for both your spiritual levels.

-=!=-

5. Just in case you are interested, I voluntarily associate myself with heterosexual interaction. The people who do this use heterosexual activity and personality-driven sexual fantasies to create pleasure within natural, loving relationships. This is a reasonable belief system that can be used to enhance a decent lifestyle, and I enjoy living it. I don't want to change.

-=!=-

6. In order for you to convert my sexuality from the one that I have chosen, and gain sex from your actions, you must disrespect my freedom of choice, crush my personality, and use overpowering force to achieve physical sexual interaction. If you attempt to do this, you will be guilty of attempted rape, and I will have no choice but to request police involvement to prevent a crime.

-=!=-

7. It is a factual belief that a vagina is designed for the purpose of being penetrated by a penis. I didn't design the system; I simply understand how to use it.

8. Owing to the fact that the skin layer on the penile helmet is porous, and that a virus can be introduced through it, in the common event that an anal sphincter develops a fissure, during anal intercourse, such a behavior will allow blood-borne diseases and other infections into my body. I consider it to be an unprofessional and dangerous risk to insert my penis into a cavity that is designed to store and excrete body waste products.

-=!=-

9. I like to believe that I am attractive enough to be selectable by other people for the purposes of having sex. In order to help my selected partner feel the same way as I do, I must employ standards, as do they. For this reason, I would like to believe that I have better than average partners. If I was to choose bisexuality, in order to maximize the number of potential sexual partners that were available, my self-respect would force me to only choose the top 25 percent of the population in terms of aesthetic beauty. Consequently, I would have to choose the best looking 50 percent of the opposite gender in order to prove that my professional optician had done his job properly.

-=!=-

10. I cannot breed naturally, without heterosexual interaction.

-=!=-

11. I like being straight.

-=!=-

12. There is a base pleasure response in the mind and body of an animal, upon the perception of a potential breeding partner. The instinctive willingness of the animal to attempt or pursue any mating activity is driven by the excitement caused during anticipation of further pleasure. Animals that do not have a complete awareness and understanding of their environment, other animals in it, and the purpose of sex are potentially vulnerable to the following mistakes: identifying a sexual partner that cannot breed and having an excitement-driven belief that any orifice will do.

-=!=-

13. Females are designed to be penetrated and therefore cannot shag each other without help.

-=!=-

14. If homosexual behavior was justified and taught to all of the next generation, the human race would be extinct in one hundred years.

-=!=-

15a. In order to promote your own personal life system, it is tempting to believe that communicating the ideas in it will assist the listener to easily convert him or her to your way of thinking. If you set up your input information, your thinking method, and a reward of congratulation for achieving the conclusion, this will be possible. This simple technique can be used on a junior or inexperienced thinkers in order to bring them to the conclusion that you have intended them to arrive at. With care and good personal skills, you can reassure them that they are correct to have learned your ideas. If you can prove that the ideas you teach are valuable to the people you are teaching, and that these ideas will stand for themselves in any mind, then you truly are being generous to the inexperienced thinkers.

15b. A word to all junior or inexperienced thinkers. Any idea, word, reason, motivation, concept, concern, or excuse that permits you to change one idea in your system of confirmed beliefs must be carefully examined. The above method is potentially used by non-heterosexuals to confuse a heterosexual for just long enough to convince you that your sexuality should be changed for your own benefit, even if only for an experiment. Once you have made the error of believing this, without understanding all of the consequences, you have failed to defend yourself in an intellectual environment!

-=!=-

A Concept Definition of Power as a Mental Tool

A concept can be defined as a theory composed of a set of ideas or beliefs. In the case of power, there are several ways to define it work divided by time, brute force (muscle power), or political influence. All three of these definitions refer to the application of energies to achieve an effect, and the time taken to achieve it dictates the magnitude. The first is a technical definition, whereas the second and third are applied to a context or environment. We need to detect some form of change in an environment to calculate whether work has been achieved, and so something in the environment must have been manipulated with forces (applied energies) for the influence to have occurred. Therefore, it is reasonable to devise a generic definition of power that refers to the application of energy to an environment in order to achieve an effect. If you consider that power can be used as a resource by a manipulating entity (such as a politician), then power provides the ability to manipulate an environment. In the case of people who have the skill required to use power safely, it could be considered as an asset which is associated with their identity, and they would then be enabled as powerful. The end result gives us the following: 'Power is the ability to manipulate an environment or an entity within it, using a mechanism, as seen from an individuals' perspective.'

If we consider this as a reasonable definition, then given any method of causing an effect with any context applied to it, we are all capable of claiming that we have the skills and resources to use power. Within this system, the main difficulty of this perception of power is to get confirmation from other individuals as to the validity of your personal power system. Things that might affect the opinion of an individual about a specific type of power include:

Whether it successfully achieves the work objective.

How efficient it is.

Whether it is socially acceptable or morally sound (i.e., petrol causes pollution, or laziness causes physical deterioration).

Is damage limitation required for this method of applying power? (That is, "Have I been reckless while using my influence?")

Does your type of power require control with a level of fidelity?

How will my power be used safely within this context?

-=!=-

A Concept Definition of
Love as a Mental Tool

A concept can be defined as a theory composed of a set of ideas or beliefs. In the case of love, there are several ways to define it.

1. To have a great fondness and affection for a person or thing.
2. To have a passionate desire for a person.
3. An intense emotion of affection, warmth, and regard towards a person or thing.
4. A deep feeling of sexual attraction and desire.
5. A beloved person.

-=!=-

Your task is to define the concept of love with a partner of your choice!

-=!=-

Techniques, that are available for use

For the purposes of this book, we seek to experience the use of sexual power, but we must do this within a loving relationship. Therefore, both parties should agree that the techniques used are acceptable and enjoyable, in order to promote pleasure for all. In order to create a satisfactory result for the partners, it would be advisable to establish a few rules. These rules convey the principles that represent the intention of the speaker.

- You must always think with the intention of producing positive results for both you and your lover.

- You must communicate your intention and your methods to your partners.

- You must allow for discussion and design alterations in order to get agreement from your partners.

- You must be responsive to the "NO" or "STOP" commands.

-=!=-

Belief Machines Personalized for "The Rock Hard Dinosaur Killer"

(Male Sex-Lovers Belief Machines Perceived from The Rock Hard Dinosaur Killer's Perspective)

The Sex God Belief Machine.

This is a qualification of experience that indicates the abilities of the holder. The holder will be aware of all available tools and resources within the system and will have full knowledge and experience of how to apply them to the full satisfaction of their partners in a personalized manner. A sex god can obliterate a woman with sex, and she will love him forever because of the gratitude that she feels for what he has given to her. Each sex god will have a trademark that will be called a gift, which will be a specific and unique fantasy that only he will be able to perform.

The Dragon's Kiss Belief Machine.

My personal belief is that the art of making love is to create beauty in the mind. When two lovers connect to concentrate their affection upon each other, they will impress feelings beyond belief into their spiritual existence. May all the women whom I have ever loved know this to be true, for as I have touched their minds with the gift of pleasure, this has always been my intention. The act of making love is a sexual ritual for a spiritual being. To the woman I would love next: May you have eyes of shattered crystal that are the centerpiece of a facial work of art. May you have a body of power and beauty and grace that is to be worshiped with awe. May you have the spirit of a silken dragon that is tempered with ecstatic love. And may you issue the kiss of an angel that lifts me to a mental state of rapture.

-=!=-

The Pretty Pussy Competition Belief Machine.

I am a judge for the skill with which my extrovert lover will show off and proffer herself in an exotic dance, for the sake of this friendly achievement amongst her peers. I wonder, who will win? The one with the biggest tits, of course!

-=!=-

The Sugar-Daddy Belief Machine.

I enjoy the feeling of knowing that my fantastic lover needs to be cared for and is a beautiful, innocent young lady inside who doesn't understand how much Sugar-Daddy needs to protect her from all the naughty boys. She's always pleased to see me and enjoys pleasing, although she has little idea how good she is at it. I let her do it because she likes it. She obviously feels good about herself when she makes me sp*nk, and she gets so excited. She loves her Sugar-Daddy's cock and doesn't need anybody else.

-=!=-

The Ladies Toy Belief Machine.

As I relax on my day off, my naughty little sluts enjoy trying to excite me with loud, expressive, sexual messages. They intentionally drive arousing signals and phrases into my brain that generate instinctive urges to sp*nk everywhere, and that I cannot control. I feel their willpower and wanton lust forcing me to relieve my urgent need for orgasm, as I desperately try not to ejaculate during my submissive masturbation reaction. Eventually, my sluts win as I pop in the head and splash my sp*nk over all of them in one massive burst.

(For a list of the things that my naughty little sluts said, see the following fantasies: Coffee and Biscuits, Bitchy Banter, Audible Rainbow, and Yes, Miss Madam, in that order.)

-=!=-

The Coffee and Biscuits Belief Machine.

A list of things that she and her mates don't mind their boyfriends overhearing when they're having a naughty chat.

(All statements are available for use with the Ladies Toy fantasy.)

"I love sitting on his cock!"

"Oh … It's more fun when you turn your back to him and squeeze his balls!"

"I love his cock when it squirts!"

"Oh … I can't resist putting it in my mouth for that!"

"I love whipping his cock with a lash made of leather!"

"Oh … I use that to dress up in so he can masturbate over my body!"

"I love him so much that I really like to turn him on by posing!"

"Oh … the reason I do that is cos it makes me cum when he masturbates!"

"I love to suck my Sugar Daddy's cock and pretend that I'm his naughty little girl!"

"Oh … In my case, since I've been Sugar Daddy's little girl, I've been naughty on his cock!"

"I love to think my husband enjoys my feet, cos I wear sexy stiletto shoes!"

"Oh … I know my husband loves my feet, cos I wave them in the air when I'm horny!"

"I love to pose naked for my man cos I know he likes to look at my pussy!"

"Oh … my man's the same. That's why I sit on his face every night!"

"I love to impress him by telling him that the dinner he cooked tasted nice."

"Oh … when mine cooks dinner, I always tell him that his cock tastes better."

"I love sitting on him until he swells up and makes my sciatic nerves tingle."

"Oh … I see what you mean. That *is* cock!"

-=!=-

The Bitchy Banter Belief Machine.

A list of things you heard when your girlfriends were arguing like naughty cock sluts about which one of them wants your cock the most.

(All statements are available for use with the Ladies Toy fantasy.)

"Why don't you stop sucking him, so that I can masturbate him with rubber gloves on?"

"Hummmmmmmmmmm!"

"It's my big cock, so give it back!"

"Not until I've emptied his balls!"

"I feel like giving my boyfriend a lesson in French kissing tonight!"

"If I staple his nose to my pussy first, you won't be able to, will you?"

"My latest beauty tip is that my boyfriend appreciates the shape of my mouth when I wear lipstick."

"When I want him to do that, I use his sp*nk."

"My attitude is that I have to get my pussy out because my boyfriend loves me!"

"I know different. My boyfriend loves me cos I get my pussy out!"

"My boyfriend has just admitted that he wants to be used to straighten out lipstick lesbians!"

"Oh, goodeey… I'm excited as shag!"

-=!=-

The Audible Rainbow Belief Machine.

A list of things for you to shout at your deaf, idiotic, kind, submissive boyfriend, specifically for his excitement and pleasure.

(All statements are available for use with the Ladies Toy fantasy.)

"When I've made you squirt, I'm gonna use your sp*nk as lipstick!"

"If you don't squirt, I'm gonna to staple your nose to my pussy!"

"Sniff my pussy, or I'll have you lick the cum out of my gusset!"

"Swallow my cum, while I blow the back of your head off with my pussy!"

"Get your cock out. I'm gonna use you to cum on!"

"I'm gonna kink you up while you're sp*nking!"

"That tasted almost as good as your cock!"

"I'm gonna stuff my knickers full of pussy and make you lick them clean!"

"I need to open my legs, cos I want to be your Wifey Slut!"

"I'm gonna whack your bell end so hard with my crop that you're gonna collapse with pleasure!"

"Let's talk while I've got my pussy out, and we can mass debate with each other!"

"I'm gonna have you force-fed on rubber teats filled with pussy juice!"

"I wanna be a total shag piece by the time you've finished using me with your cock, sir!"

"I'm gonna squirt my cum down your japsii!"

"Lick my heels and sp*nk!"

"Persecuting you with my pussy—sounds like fun!"

"I'm gonna make you sp*nk so much that you're gonna waddle like a duck!"

"You deserve a slap in the face with my pussy!"

"I'm gonna make you sp*nk in my pussy!"

"I'm gonna discipline your cock for not sp*nking!"

"I'm gonna give you so much nursey treatment that you're gonna think you're sick!"

"I'm gonna use you like a whore uses a sex toy to make her pussy wet!"

"I'm gonna turn you into a sex robot and control you like shag!"

"I want you to enjoy masturbating while I wipe my pussy on you until you sp*nk!"

"Me and my sister are gonna play pussy splat on your cock!"

"I'm gonna straddle you when I feel like squirting my cum everywhere!"

"When my mouth feels empty, I'm gonna use your cock to play suck and squirt!"

"Wifey wants to give you a tit-shag blow-job right now!"

"I'm gonna lash your cock until you're shagged!"

"If you don't sp*nk, I'm gonna smash your brain with pussy!"

"The next time you try to sp*nk, I'm gonna paralyze your brain with nipple worship!"

"I wanna grip your balls to stop you sp*nking while I suck you until your head pops!"

"I'm gonna give you cock discipline until you can't sp*nk any more!"

"I'm gonna whack your balls with my whip while I make you eat my cum!"

"I'm going to pussy spray all over my sex tools and make you lick them clean!"

"Shut up—you're just about to get shagged!"

"Wifey's going to parade her squirting pussy until you can't stop masturbating!"

"I'm gonna lick your balls until they're empty!"

"I'm gonna have you fitted with testicle 'expanders'!"

"I'm gonna use my stilettos like spurs to force your cock up my pussy!"

"I'm gonna make you lick my c*m out of my pussy!"

"I'm gonna give you a nuclear power blow-job!"

"I'm gonna give you a brain spasm with my tongue!"

"I'm gonna 'lesbianize' you with my strap-on!"

"If you think I'm only gonna make you squirt once, you're stupid!"

"I'm gonna tie you up so you can't masturbate, and I'll make you watch lesbian incest!"

"I'm gonna invite lots of pretty lesbians to a rubber stocking party in your head!"

"I'm gonna use your skull as a pussy squirt receptacle until you admit you enjoy it!"

"When I see you, my pussy gets wet and I want to be shagged!"

"I love your cock, Sugar Daddy. It makes me want to spread-eagle my legs!"

"I'm gonna lash your cock while I masturbate it until you empty your balls!"

"When I've finished with you, the only thing you'll remember is how to eat my cum!"

"I'm gonna insert a drinking straw into your japsii and suck your balls dry!"

"I'm gonna make you want to masturbate while I give your cock a bitch whacking!"

"Me and my six-foot beauty queen lesbian mates are gonna hammer you with sex tools!"

"My pussy-filled knickers are damp enough to sniff while you wear them on your head!"

"I know you love me, and that's why I decided to be your sp*nk slut!"

"If your cock leaks when I squeeze your balls, I'm gonna reclassify you as kinky!"

"If you squirt less than a pint when I de-sp*nk you, you're a wimp!"

-=!=-

The Yes, Miss Madam Belief Machine.

A list of things for you and your slutty sub-missives to agree to, when your lover gives out orders and suggestions.

(All statements are available for use with the Ladies Toy fantasy.)

"Shag the sluts while I squeeze your balls!"

"Ladies, get out your riding crops. It's time for target practice on his cock!"

"Let's all squirt our pussies on his reflex point!"

"We all want his cock. Let's share him out"

"We're gonna persecute you with our pussies!"

"Let's gag him with pussy and take his cock in turns!"

"Now we're gonna lick your balls until they're empty!"

"We're gonna suck you off with our pussies in your face!"

"We now maintain you as a female prostitutes' dummy!"

"We're gonna use you as a personal satisfaction device!"

"Cum in her mouth!"

"All of us cock obsessed sluts want your sp*nk!"

"Now we're gonna make you shag us all together!"

"Lick up all our girlie cum!"

"My mates want to shag you, and I'm gonna to let 'em!"

"Enjoy all of our sex!"

"We're gonna have you wired up next week, so you can't stop sp*nking!"

"Let's take turns at straddling his cock!"

-=!=-

The Beach Party Belief Machine.

The waterproof sheet lay shimmering in the light breeze as we put pebbles on each corner. As we stripped down to our birthday suits, the sun oil came out of the rucksack, and we rubbed each other down for protection. All of my life partners were there, and as soon as we touched each other, we realized that it was about time that we consummated our group relationship. The sun oil ritual began as we gently maneuvered into a slippery mass of young and beautiful bodies, caressing and flirting with our lovers' most sensuous parts. I felt myself get stiff and started to feel the attentions of all my lovers, one by one. There was kissing and shagging, wanking and sucking all over our sleek bodies for at least an hour, until each of them had taken their turn at cumming over my cock. With one final gesture of a delirious orgasm, I had come to the satisfying conclusion of the love consummation ceremony.

-=!=-

The Consuming Desires Belief Machine, Part One.

My fantastic lover and I were sitting down and teasing the talent one night whilst watching a film called *Nine and a Half Weeks*. When we realized what the main characters were doing in the kitchen scene, we started to imagine how we could create a similar event in our bedroom, for the sake of spicing up our love life. After a few minutes of deliberation, we each thought we had outdone the other with our idea of what edible substance we could introduce into our sex routines. Both of us were smiling at each other with ideas in our heads, and because we didn't want to ruin the effect, we chose to discuss the health and safety aspect of how we should approach this new fantasy. The first sensible idea I came up with was that if either of us needed to launch ourselves into the air whilst swinging off the chandelier, it would be a good practice to wear a motorcycle crash helmet. My lover responded by introducing the concept of a plastic dust sheet to be placed over the sheets to protect them from all the blood that was going to be splashed about while she was beating me up for being so stupid. After a while, we finished by having a laugh with words and decided to get down to the sexy bit.

She told me to wait for five minutes before coming upstairs to the bedroom so that she could be ready for me when I arrived. During the five minutes, I went to the fridge and collected the article of food with which I had decided to surprise her. I then went up the stairs. As I walked into the bedroom with the food in my hand, I was pleasantly surprised to see my lover laying naked on the bed with her hair tied up and her body glistening with some form of oil smothered all over it. She looked very sexy because she had shaven herself earlier that afternoon. I had already undressed in order to impress her with my willingness to participate in bedroom games, and so it was easy for her to rub the coconut oil over my whole body. While she did this, I couldn't help noticing the feelings of low friction slipperiness on my skin, and I started to imagine a sensual session of me sliding all over her body for fun. Little was

I expecting my adventurous lover to tell me that we had to lick each other clean before we were allowed to have sex. With the sexy thought of personal cleansing in our minds, we spent half an hour performing oral worship on each others' beautiful bodies before we shagged ourselves senseless for a laugh.

-=!=-

The Consuming Desires Belief Machine, Part Two.

My fantastic lover and I were lying in bed with happy smiles on our faces and the thought of what we had just done to each other in our minds. With the everlasting desire for self-improvement and further achievement at the forefront of my thoughts, I leaned over to the bedside cabinet and reached for the tin of spray cream. As I retrieved it from the cabinet, I pulled back the sheet to reveal my erect cock, and I rolled my foreskin back to allow the helmet to show. This caught my lover's attention, and she watched as I quietly sprayed the cream all over the helmet with a smile on my face. "What are you expecting me to do with that?" she said as she tried not to laugh too much. "It's my turn to choose now!" I said as I looked her in the eye.

Other Womens' Comments
That The Rock Hard Dinosaur Killer Likes to Hear

-=!=-

"You're cock's massive!"

"You have a masculine Adam's apple!"

"Every time I look at you, I empty my pussy into my knickers!"

"The power in your cock is unbelievable!"

"When you shag me, I cum everywhere!"

"Evolution says it's natural selection to let you shag me!"

"I'm gonna wail like a banshee when you make me cum!"

"You excite me so much, my pussy wants to squeak!"

"Get inside me and enjoy yourself!"

"I will, I do, and I have!"

"I'm wearing this for you, sir!"

"Would you like the rubber or the silk gloves, sir?"

"Would you like the leather or the lace gloves, sir?"

"Corrrr!, that's nice and hard!"

"Please, can I have your shag, sir!"

"When you sp*nk in me, my head pops inside!"

"I really love you cos your cock's so big!"

"You've got an education and a big cock, and I like that about you!"

"I would be proud to swallow all of it, sir!"

"I can't get your cock out of my head!"

"You could start a bitch fight with that cock!"

"My pussy feels tight with you in it!"

"I like being nice to you, cos you make my pussy wet!"

"I'm gonna have a laugh on your cock in a minute!"

"Oh, Sugar Daddy, I need a fanny tickler, cos I haven't cum yet!"

"I want to be shagged by a powerful man, and I think you're the one!"

"Please, sir, can you shave me?"

"I can't help it, sir. I love your sp*nk!"

"Sugar Daddy, please, can you use me as a toy?"

"Thank you, sir. I love a good pussy filling!"

"I bet you could shag me good, couldn't you?"

"I thought I was powerful until I met you!"

"I love you, sir. I'm yours!"

"Sugar Daddy, I haven't seen one that big before!"

"I want more!"

"I've got a tiny little pussy, sir. Would you like some?"

"My cute pussy needs some sp*nk. Will you do it for me?"

"I'd have a bitch fight over your cock any day!"

"I can't help getting randy when you touch me up!"

"If you tell me you love me, my legs open wider!"

"Saying 'I love you, slut!' makes me swallow, sir!"

"Are you the one who empties womens' pussies?"

"When I've finished wanking you off, my sister's gonna lick you clean!"

"I've decided to have a man in my life … and it's you!"

-=!=-

Belief Machines Personalized for Female Team Members

(Female Sex-Lovers' Belief Machines Perceived from the Rock Hard Dinosaur Killer's Perspective)

-=!=-

The Sex Goddess Belief Machine.

This woman must be admired with awe. She has a qualification of experience that allows her to develop high-impact fantasies. The holder will be aware of all available tools and resources within the system, and she will have full knowledge and experience of how to apply them to the full satisfaction of her partner in a personalized manner. A sex goddess can obliterate a man with sex, and he will love her forever because of the gratitude that he feels for what she has given to him. Each sex goddess will have a trademark that will be called a gift, which will be a specific and unique fantasy that only she will be able to perform.

-=!=-

The Forced Submissive Worship and Orgasm Belief Machine.

My fantastic lover is a powerful female telepath, and she has a sex drive to match. She likes nothing more than to burst my brain with stunning pleasure commands and signals when she feels like using me as a sex object. First she arouses me by instructing her twenty-two-year-old third cousin to parade around with her tight little pussy in full view, and to make me clean it with my tongue. She never lets me relieve myself as she winds me up with full-force "Do it" messages, like "Put your tongue on her clit" and "Swallow!" She always makes me shag the little slut with her massive rubber-clad tits in my mouth. When she decides to make me unload my sp*nk, she likes to whip my balls while she stuns my brain with her constant, maximum-force, powerfully exciting commands to sp*nk. It paralyzes me as she sends them in repeatedly, so that all I can do is squirt ounces of fluid into her third cousin as she wriggles her spraying pussy down on my cock forcefully and repeats the words, "I love you, Sugar Daddy!" I love my awesome lover and her extrovert third cousin too.

-=!=-

The Blokey Banter Belief Machine.

Things that all the girls like to hear from their dominant male when they need a good talking to:

(All statements provided by female team members.)

"After I've sp*nked over your tits, I'm gonna use you till you're shagged!"

"Get your pussy out! Sugar Daddy wants one!"

"I just came on your breakfast!"

"Get on the bed and look sexy!"

"Be quiet, or I'll gag you on my cock!"

"Now you've made me squirt like that, you're gonna have to lick my cock clean!"

"Are you thinking about my cock? Cos I like that in a woman!"

"Come here, you! I wanna shag!!"

"I'm gonna shag you like a Sex Robot Shagging Machine!"

"If you wanna feel power, you just sit on this!"

"For your birthday I'm gonna dress up like a Teletubby and shag you!"

"Get ready … I'm gonna use you to shag on!"

"I've got so much sp*nk for your blow-job, you're gonna need to throw up to get the second half in!"

"I'm your personal sex machine!"

"I'm gonna walk you round the room with a collar and lead, making you cum on things."

"It's your job to take my sp*nk on command."

"You and I seriously need to shag!"

"Not only are you going to be my bitch, you're going to be a happy bitch!"

"Every morning, I'm gonna lick your pussy until you open your legs wide enough to be shagged!"

"I let my lover dominate me because it gives her a sense of power."

"The reason we are equals in this relationship is because I say so!"

"I'm gonna teach you to use my sp*nk as lipstick!"

"By the time I've finished with you, the only thing you'll remember is how to eat my sp*nk!"

"I'm gonna blow the back of your head off with my sp*nk!"

"I'm gonna touch you, and you're gonna feel beautiful!"

"Stop shaggin' about, and get your pussy out!"

"Oi, sluts! Why don't you sort me out some cuddly feelings?"

"If you're nice to me, I will show you God through orgasm!"

-=!=-

The Power Pussy Belief Machine.

My fantastic lover is a rampant girlie when she gets out her pussy. She enjoys rubbing her silk stockings on my cock as she strides over my supine body to get her legs apart. She knows what those high-heeled shoes do to me, and she gets off in her head when she straddles down and forces my throbbing cock up her beautiful, moist, shaven pussy. I love her thrusting up and down on it as she encourages me to sp*nk inside her. The dominant slut enjoys feeling my cock swell in her pussy, and she rides me faster. I can't stop myself from moaning out loud as my head rushes, and my sp*nk squirts again and again until my balls ache with emptiness. This woman can blow my head off with her pussy, and I love her for it.

-=!=-

The More Pussy Belief Machine.

My fantastic lover knows that I'm an "I see, I want" kind of guy. She also knows that ideas have the same effect on me. I like it when she whispers the idea of "more pussy" into my head because I want to get harder and shag more. As my mind excitedly and repetitively accelerates on "more pussy" and "shag harder"', she whispers the words into my head again and again. With her legs open and her pleasure exposed, she drives my instinctive excitement until I can feel my sp*nk rising into her pretty femininity. She laughs as we collapse into a heap of sweaty, happy flesh and bone on the bed.

-=!=-

The Girl Power Belief Machine.

One day, my lover came home early from work and caught me having a wank in the bedroom. She walked in on me quite unexpectedly and I didn't notice her do it because I was so busy. "Hello, darling. What are you doing?" she said, knowing full well. I startled and froze. "Don't be embarrassed," she said. "Just tell me why you feel the need, when you have a lover." I didn't know what to say, other than "I had an urgent need to sp*nk and I've just ended up frustrating myself. I think my balls are empty!"

"Oh," she said. "Well, I'm your lover, and I'm only too happy to sort you out. I've got just the plan for stopping frustrated balls." I was pleasantly surprised at her reaction, and I got out of bed. That evening, after I had gotten over the shock of revealing my desires to my lover, I had to explain to her that I felt like a bad lover because I didn't know how to express my needs to her. After a long conversation, she said, "I can sort this out with a phone call." She drew her battle plan in the kitchen and told me not to listen. Sometime later, she came in to the front room and said that she had decided to enroll in a group of women who had the same difficulty with their lovers, and the group was on its way for their first meeting. She suggested that I get an early night and let her see what they could come up with, and so I went to the bedroom and got into bed. I'd only been in bed for ten minutes when the doorbell rang. I wondered what was going on. It wasn't long before all four of her mates were in the front room discussing me, and I didn't have a clue what to expect. After about half an hour of trying to listen to them (unsuccessfully), I heard my lover walking up the corridor in her stilettos. Those shoes really catch my attention. Then I heard more footsteps with exactly the same clicking. As the bedroom door opened, the lights came on, and I looked up at the five women entering their new play area, each wearing a black sheen rubber, three-quarter-length catsuit and carrying a twenty-four-inch riding crop. There were whoops of excitement coming from the other four as my lover said, "We've just decided what wanking technique we're going to use, and you're going to be disciplined into sp*nking correctly!" With that, all five women crowded round the bed and started giving me commands to open my legs and wank. It was a real turn-on to see all their feminine forms as they pranced around like dominatrices and disciplined my balls and my cock head with their riding crops. As they did this, I played with myself under their correctional instruction. My inhibitions dropped while I watched my lover join in with the other four sexy minxes, and they teased me and taunted me with their exciting shouts. "Give me your sp*nk, you hunk!" "We know how to empty our man's balls!" It was as exciting as shag, and they pushed me and urged me to wank faster and shoot my load. They organized themselves around the bed so that they could discipline me from all angles with their whips in a synchronized fashion, and I felt the fluid rising in my cock as they relentlessly struck my cock head. Eventually, I couldn't hold back any longer, and so I urgently squirted hot, sticky sp*nk all over their shiny uniforms and collapsed back on to the bed, gasping for breath. The girls giggled and pranced around, excited at what they had just made me do. My lover leaned over me with her ample breasts and gorgeous smile. Then she said, "Now that you have experienced us as a discipline and correction team, you're a good boyfriend for enjoying the gift I have given you!"

-=!=-

The Slut Shag Belief Machine.

My fantastic lover can be a slut when she gets the words "I want" in her brain. When it happens, she always wants my sp*nk. She likes to turn her back on me and straddle my stiff, swollen cock as she uses her riding crop to whip my balls. I love it and enjoy her forcing my sp*nk up her beautiful, wet pussy. My urges to squirt in her gradually overpower me as she constantly issues her demands to satisfy her lust for my fluids, and I melt into a shag-fest of orgasm. I need my slut shag of a lover.

-=!=-

The Discipline and Correction Mistress Belief Machine.

My fantastic lover gets excited when I get my cock out, because she's so proud of her skill at making me sp*nk. I like to wind her up by telling her that I don't think she will be able to tonight because I've had too much sex lately. I normally use the excuse that I've just spent an hour shagging her twenty-two-year-old third cousin, and I couldn't help shooting most of my fluid over her massive tits because they are so much bigger and more attractive than my lover's. To add to the fun, I usually wait until my lover hasn't had any cock for a while, and she really wants it. She always swallows the bait and goes shagging mental. I enjoy seeing my lover in high-energy animation.

At this point she quite rightly decides that she desperately needs to assert discipline and correction treatment on my cock. This is when she pushes my wrists into the two pairs of handcuffs that we keep hanging off the bed frame for just such occasions. As she's looking through the bedside cabinet for her lash, she starts saying things like, "I might have to staple your nose to my pussy for that!" Things like that make me excited and hard. The slut knows she's having that effect on my cock with her words. Confident that she has the physical advantage, she straddles me and makes me gasp with pleasure as she disciplines my cock with the lash—one firm strike after another on the gland whilst demanding my sp*nk. She keeps stunning my cock, and I feel a turmoil of positive emotion rise within my mind and body as my mental state energizes into ecstasy. The nerve stimulation is fantastic. Eventually, my fluids squirt everywhere and my head pops. My mind state collapses into euphoric gratitude for having been corrected by my lover. That's when she unlocks the handcuffs, and we have a loving, satisfied cuddle.

-=!=-

The Queen of Domination Blow-jobs Belief Machine.

My fantastic lover knows that I sometimes get shy about the inhibitions in my mind when I try to masturbate for her satisfaction. She blasts them out of my skull by using her dominant attitude and her lash on the end of my cock. As she lashes and sucks the gland, she masturbates the shaft, and my throbbing, excited balls tense up. I feel her stimulate the head of my cock with the lash for my pleasure. I love it when she forces the orgasm into me with her overpowering lust for a state of mutual sexual bliss and her orders to release my sp*nk. It makes my lover happy to feel me uncontrollably squirt fluid into her mouth. I admire the power of my lover's ambition to beat any prospective competition.

-=!=-

The One Good Goblin Belief Machine.

My fantastic lover is so mischievous. She's forever tickling the end of my cock with her tongue when I'm trying to sleep. Mind you, I don't stop her because I enjoy it. She likes to see how far she can push her tiny little tongue in to my japsii while she's thinking about keeping her lover happy.

-=!=-

The Forced Masturbation Belief Machine.

My fantastic lover gets frustrated when I haven't sp*nked in her for a while. It makes her feel like rubbing herself and ordering me to watch. She likes to turn me on by opening her legs and letting me see her fingers slide into her lingerie. I enjoy it when she relieves herself into her hand; it makes me hard, and I want to play with myself. When I do, she climbs up on me and stuffs her pussy-filled knickers into my face. Then she demands that I sniff her hot, wet crotch. I like it and can't stop myself from masturbating harder and faster as I watch her rub her frustrated clitoris through the g-string. I love it when she constantly orders me to wank and sp*nk for her. It makes my balls throb, and I want to shoot my load. The best time for me to empty my balls is when her orders get louder and more urgent. The more excited she gets, the more my balls tense up, because we both know that she's about to make me lick up her pussy juice as it squirts into the tight, silky material that I'm sniffing. It always makes me squirt hard when my lover excites me with her lust.

-=!=-

The Kink Trip Belief Machine.

My fantastic lover likes to wipe her pussy on things and make me lick them clean. Last time she did it, she stopped off at the sex shop on her way from work and bought a blow-up doll. As she walked in the door, she smiled at me and said, "I've got a nice surprise for you." I expectantly grinned without knowing what she had planned. Later on that evening, she disappeared for a while as I was watching telly, and I barely noticed that she had gone. Some more time passed, and then I started to hear gentle moaning noises coming from the bedroom. I couldn't help liking the sound of her playing on her own, but I wondered why she hadn't invited me. I got up and peered through the gap in the bedroom door, and to my amazement, there was my lover wearing a strap-on dildo and shagging the blow-up doll in the missionary position. She looked up at me and smiled as she said, "Hello, lover. I've decided I'm bisexual, and we're having a threesome tonight." I stepped further into the room with a fun smile on my face. "I see you're the dominant half of the relationship, then," I said. "Can I join in?" My lover smiled as she climbed off the dolly and said, "So you want to find out what your surprise is?"

"Yes, please!" I said. My lover grinned at me and knowingly said, "I've just cum on her tits. Why don't you let me watch you wank your cock off while you lick them clean, and I'll give her a proper pussy spanking for refusing to cum?"

-=!=-

The Wifey Slut Belief Machine.

My fantastic lover has a powerful maternal instinct. When I cuddle up on her ample breasts at night, she gets lots of broody female thoughts in her head, and her body starts to react. Her pussy gets hot, and her breasts swell up as her nipples start to sweat. I can't resist putting my mouth on them and tasting the sweet perspiration. It makes her moan gently. I need to shag her when she's moaning, and she always opens her pussy nice and wide for my immense hard-on. We just can't help enjoying each other. When I sp*nk, my wifey slut is always so happy and satisfied that it makes me feel euphoric, and I want to shag her again and again with her nipples in my mouth.

-=!=-

The Nipple Worship Belief Machine.

My fantastic lover has incredible tits. Her nipples jut out half an inch, and I can't stop staring at them when she strips off her top. I particularly love it when we go sunbathing. I can never hold back my enthusiasm when I think of her gently smothering her breasts in shiny, slippery oil. It makes me want to rub my cock up and down between them. I like watching as she rolls them around in her hands and feels herself stiffen up in those tasty erogenous zones. The good thing is, she likes being watched, and she wets her knickers with pussy juice as she shows off in the sun.

The Nipples and Silk Belief Machine.

My fantastic lover deserves pleasure just for being mine. Since I met her, I have learned to use her nipples to control her into orgasm. While she's doing the washing up in the evening, I like to sneak up behind her and give her a sensuous cuddle. As I put my arms around her, I like to stroke my hands over her nipples and feel them through her silk blouse. The cool, smooth silk gently slides across them, and she smiles at the thought of being touched. I can't help enjoying them with the delicate teasing movements of my fingers as she arches her back as if to accept me for a shag. It turns me on to know that my woman is effectively under my control because she likes to submit to the gentle stimulation that I know how to put into her body. It arouses her to let me massage them until her feminine pussy gets damp. She is very sensitive, and it's easy to make her cum, but it's more fun to tell her not to. As she tries to restrain her pelvic muscles from tightening, I like to wind her up even further and keep instructing her to relax. I always know when she's close to the point when she can't hold back anymore, because she breathes so fast and tilts her head back on to my shoulder. That's when I whisper into her ear, "Do it now … Cum!" I get a fantastic kick out of ordering her to release, knowing that she can't help but respond by flooding her knickers. I think she's glad she met me too, but I'm not sure if she likes the fact that I never do the washing up.

-=!=-

The Sex and Love Robot Belief Machine.

I love my darlin' lover! Her feminine form is so sleek that whenever I see her, my eyes slide all over her body until they get to her beautiful pussy. It makes me want to treat her like a sex robot love machine, by walking her around the room with a collar and lead, making her cum on things and take my sp*nk on command. She's very submissive and doesn't mind one bit when I use her to sp*nk on. I love to see her in her favorite black stilettos and a soft leather collar, which tells her she is mine. As I clip the lead to her delicate throat, I enjoy whispering in to her ear some of the beliefs that we share about the beauty of submission. I know that in her mind, she is a wild and free lover and needs me to temper her spirit with gentle control. The mind lock in her head is associated with her orgasm, and she knows that it cannot be released without my command.

As I guide her on to the dildo stool, I carefully maneuver her into position with my words. I order her to slide herself onto the stool and take the toy into herself, with her shoes splayed apart and her back arched. It is a joy to see her accept the pleasure that comes from my instruction. We can spend hours of pleasure locked in this power imbalance, while I feel her warm, sweet lips worship me orally. Every so often, I get a kick out of giving her the command to cum, and she does. When I feel the need for relief, I order her to suck more assertively and swallow my orgasm.

The Pole Dancer Belief Machine.

I was a naughty little boy once upon a time. That's how I decided whom I would like to marry. One night I went to a strip club and watched a woman pole dancing. Her body was a perfect example of the female form. As I was transfixed on her exciting movements, my mind started ticking over about how I was going to get her. The whole audience was enjoying the show, and I needed to gain an advantage over all the other eager men who hadn't had any pussy lately. This woman was worth the contents of my wallet, and so at the end of her performance, I called to the manager and requested a private show. He quickly ushered me into a private curtained area and poured me a drink while he explained that she would be available in a few minutes. As he left to get her, I sat in the firm comfortable sofa and started to wait with anticipation. My waiting soon came to an end when she slid into the room from behind the curtain after enough time to change her outfit. She was stunning, and she knew it. Her confidence was amazing. Without saying a word, she started to writhe her body in the most luxurious, sexy manner. I felt myself stiffening as she captured my gaze with her movements. It was against club rules to touch her, which made me want her even more. In an attempt to attract her intentions for my hopes of a future life with such a woman, I decided to guide her attention towards my personality with a gentlemanly offer. "Just in case I cannot hold myself back from reaching out, would you like to tie my hands?" I offered. She giggled as she carried on dancing and said, "Don't worry about that. It's my pleasure to take care of all your needs this evening." She seductively moved to the chair and gently touched our bodies together. I was amazed to find myself feeling orgasmic in seconds. As I relaxed in the chair with joy in my mind and body, she quietly slipped out of the room. That will always stay in my memory with my future fantasies.

-=!=-

The Loved Woman Belief Machine.

My fantastic lover is so pure and innocent in her need for affection. I feel masculine when she asks me to cuddle her. I want her to feel loved and protected when she's close. We enjoy seeing each other happy. I like it when she hasn't got a worry in the world, and she starts to get giggly and playful on my cock. She loves to tease and please her Sugar Daddy with her mouth and tongue. She doesn't even need to excite me. Contact with her gives us mutual pleasure until we orgasm.

The Darlin' Girl Belief Machine.

My fantastic lover feels so seductive to me when she relaxes in bed. As she stretches and reaches out for me, I like the sensation of our skin touching and the feeling of being welcomed by a beautiful woman. Her warm, sensitive body is so appealing between the crisp satin sheets. I always feel my cock harden as she slides across the bed to get close to her Sugar Daddy, and I can't help myself from climbing up on to her supine body. She naturally exposes her womanhood by drawing her sexy feet apart when I do that. Sometimes she likes to wear her stockings and bedroom shoes because she thinks they're horny, but I don't mind whether she does or not, as long as she gives a deep moan when I penetrate her. When she feels me pushing into her, it turns her head on to the fact that I take care of all her needs, and it reminds her of how a grown woman can feel like a protected child. As she extends her arms around me, she whispers into my ear,

"I want your sp*nk, Sugar Daddy! Darlin' Girl needs to feel her cum squirting! Please shag me, Sugar Daddy. I want to squirt my cum all over your cock!" She never lets me down and always feels my sp*nk unloading deep into her as we orgasm for each other, together.

-=!=-

The Joy Popping Belief Machine.

My fantastic lover is aroused by my need to feel her sexual pleasure, and we often lay together, relishing each others desires as she relaxes into my thoughts. I revel in my masculine prowess as my imagination takes possession of her body by stimulating her nipples and clitoris with positive joy-popping signals. As I gently accelerate her urges to reach climax by operating the nerves in her erogenous areas, she feels seduced by my assertive intentions. The intensity of her mental state responds by increasing from pleasure to happiness and then to joy. She finally pops in her head and orgasms in her body as we relax with satisfaction in our minds and our hearts, having experienced the euphoria of love.

-=!=-

The Poetry to the Eye Belief Machine.

My fantastic lover enjoys seeing me captivated as I gaze at the flowing beauty of her movement. I feel pleasure and amazement while her image becomes the sole driving force in my mind for the production of pleasure. My lover's body is a symbol of divine, artistic creation.

-=!=-

The Fun Shag Belief Machine.

My fantastic lover is a mischievous little tart. She likes to talk sexy when she wants a shag, and it always works. She waits until I desperately lose self-control and start masturbating before she parades her beautiful body in my direction. By the time she has wound me up with her flirting and sexy talk, it's obvious I want her to satisfy me, and she enjoys using my cock as a pussy filler. I like taking her from behind while she stands bent over the kitchen table with her stockings and stilettos on. I feel loved when she begs me to sp*nk inside her. She needs it, and it's my privilege to give her as much as I can. I feel glorious when she squeals with delight as my balls empty, and sp*nk squirts out of my cock head and deep into her.

-=!=-

The Tongue and Nerve Blow-job Belief Machine.

My fantastic lover knows that this fantasy cleaning service is for submissive girls who like to lick and sniff cock while they touch and feel testicles. It's fun. She likes to see how many times she can make my cock twitch with her mouth before squeezing my balls so hard that I have to squirt my sp*nk into the back of her throat.

-=!=-

The Shag and Squirt Belief Machine.

My fantastic lover can't get enough of my cock inside her tiny, tight pussy. I love it when she gets horny and excited, because she's so cute and shag-able. I order her to get on all fours naked, so that I can watch her arch her spine and proffer her perfect shaven pussy in my direction. She knows how to turn me on with it. It makes me hard to know she needs my cock rammed into her, which is just what I'm about to do. Taking her doggy style is great because I can thrust into her and feel her tense up inside as she begs for more. I feel masculine when she cums on my cock, and then I keep shagging until my sp*nk squirts up inside her. It feels good to empty every last squirt into her, and she enjoys it.

-=!=-

The Getting-Sugar Daddy Off Belief Machine.

"I'm gonna make you sniff my pussy while I play with it! Get your cock out! I love you!"

-=!=-

The Yo-Yo Gym Dance Belief Machine.

My fantastic lover is a yo-yo dancer. She looks so good when she gymnastically parades her beautiful, young body across the dance floor. I love the pillar box red and electric blue flashes on her brilliant white three-quarter-length leotard as they blur in the bright light with quick movements. She spins her brightly colored yo-yos with excellent effect as she prances in rhythm and time. Her flirty hands dart silently in my mind and attract my attention even more. Her gymnastic prowess shows itself to the full as she athletically energizes herself through my perception. I am fascinated by her youth and vigor as she entices my mind to sexually fantasize about her. She enjoys the attention as I imagine her dancing on my cock like a ballerina beauty queen.

-=!=-

The Irresistible Fetish Mistress Belief Machine.

For the purposes of male servicing, my lover enjoys feeling me want her. She dons the kinkiest outfits and behaves in the most seductive and horny ways, while my cock gets harder and harder. As we play together, I feel like giving her feminine, damp pussy a light spanking so that it will tingle as much as my cock head. With this sort of kink trip fascinating our merged minds, I prefer to enjoy the pleasure as long as possible instead of sp*nking.

-=!=-

The Cock-obsessed Blow-job Belief Machine.

My fantastic lover knows that this testicle-emptying service is for dominant girls who want a good, hard cock obsession in their minds. The longer it's in their heads, the more urgently they need to empty my balls of sp*nk so they can get high on swallowing male fluid like proper women. She loves obsessing on pleasure with my cock gorged into her mouth up to the back of her throat, whilst squeezing my balls and masturbating the shaft. There is no doubt that she is taking my cock because she wants to enjoy it in her head and her mouth at the same time. She then forces my fluid to rise deep into her sex hungry and thirsty mouth as she stifles her moans of satisfaction on my cock. She always gets an explosive mental orgasm as she swallows my fluid when it hits the back of her throat. She loves popping her brain on my sp*nk.

-=!=-

The Pussy Love Belief Machine.

My fantastic lover has spent years honing her expert knowledge of how to drive me crazy with sex, and she devises more fantastic bedroom games. She knows how to use both our bodies as athletic and exciting sex machines by acting on my desires and immersing herself in the pleasure she gets from knowing that she is in control. We both enjoy servicing her pussy, and she never fails to make me squirt like a fountain as a reward. The last time we had a session, she gave me a nice surprise with her new outfit. As I came into the bedroom from the shower, she caught my attention with the words, "Hello Baby! Are you ready for some pussy love?" I looked at her standing by the wardrobe. She had bought herself a nice pair of sexy, high-heeled stilettos, and she'd acquired a gorgeous pair of elbow-length silk gloves that felt soft to the touch. Together with a pair of silk stockings and a skimpy suspender belt, the outfit caused her to look and feel sensational. She was wearing nothing else, and with all her limbs covered, it accentuated her slinky athletic torso and all its amazingly well-defined muscle. I felt a twinge of excitement in my head, and my cock twitched.

She moved towards me like a catwalk model and started to touch me. As her nipples gently glided across mine, she said, "You're gonna sp*nk up like a fountain when I finish you off." With that, she gently pushed me in to a sitting position on the bed. Her beautiful pussy was all I wanted to look at, and she knew exactly how submissive I am to the luxurious pleasures she can give me with it. She enthusiastically touched herself with her pussy in open view for my pleasure, for a long while. She knew that my cock was rock hard because of her. The she lifted one knee, used it to force me down on the bed, and said, "Open your mouth. I'm gonna cum like shag! Do it!" She swiveled around and stuffed my face full of derriere and pussy while she masturbated a full-force female ejaculation, which lasted for ever and surged down my throat. I gripped the sexy stilettos by the heels and gorged myself on her swollen gushing mound as she used her other hand to grip and wank my cock into her mouth. Just before I got to the point of no return, I felt her take her gagging mouth off my cock and say, "Now I'm gonna make you squirt like a fountain!"

-=!=-

The Powerful Demonstration of Love Belief Machine.

"I care about you!" she said in a silky, romantic and chocolate voice. "You're my personal shag, and I need you. I can't help it because your sp*nk turns me on."

-=!=-

The Wank Bitch Belief Machine.

My fantastic lover made me feel like a man when she became my schoolgirl sweetheart. As a boy of eighteen, I used to fantasize about the best-looking girl in my maths class, and I often fell asleep at night with her in my mind. At one point, I was so infatuated by her image that I couldn't help staring at her during the lessons. Little did I know that she was quietly offended by this, and I was confused as to why she occasionally rejected my attempts at conversation on the playground. One day, I was all dressed up in my Lycra cycling gear, ready to enter the annual school cycling competition. I was walking to the track when she appeared from behind the gym in her netball uniform. She ran straight into me. As she fell to the floor and landed with her legs splayed, I stared in amazement at her beauty. She was naked under her short, ruffled netball skirt, which had ridden up to her waist. As we both stared, our eyes slid over each others' bodies until we found the decency to force eye contact. We were both turned on by the experience. Not knowing what else to do, I leaned forward and offered her my hand to help her get up. She took it, and we pulled towards each other until our bodies were touching. She smiled. "Would you like to watch me win the race?" I said. "Okay, but I'll have to skip netball." Later that afternoon, after I had won the race with her actively cheer-leading at the side of the track, we arrived at the changing rooms and found that they were empty. As she realized that nobody was listening, she turned to me and said, "I like boys like you ... because you have power in your body." As I realized what she meant, I felt my cock swell into the object of her sexual desire. "Don't think you're getting everything," she said with a smile, and she watched me eagerly peel my cycling shorts down my legs and lay on one of the benches. I felt a tiny amount of surprise when she reached forward with her right hand and grasped hold of my swollen, stiff cock. "You've got a massive cock!" she said as her hand started to move up and down the shaft. It felt lovely as she repeatedly slid my foreskin over my helmet. I relaxed as best I could, but my balls were getting tighter with every stroke of her hand, and she saw my urgency in the expression on my face. "I really like you ... I've fancied you for ages," I said. She smiled a bit more and replied, "What you gonna do about it, huh?" With the provocative attitude in her speech, and the excitement in my mind, I couldn't help but release a full load of sp*nk all over her delicate hand. That was when I asked her to be my woman.

-=!=-

The 69 Pleasures Belief Machine.

My fantastic lover uses me to clean the pussy juice off her clit when she wants to have fun. She always acts like a submissive cock tart when she's happy. She likes to wear shiny catsuits, or a basque and stockings, while she gets her favorite Sugar Daddy extra hard. She likes nothing better than to climb on to it and suck with her pussy exposed for cleaning in the 69 position. I love it when she rubs her shaven, wet pussy on my nose and begs me to give her oral satisfaction between gulps on my shaft. The more excited she gets, the more I can hear her gagging herself on its hardness. This cock tart has orgasm on the brain as I push pleasure into her clit with my tongue and feel hers dancing on my gland. With the skill of an expert, she orchestrates our orgasms to come together, and we both squirt our entire loads of fluid into each others' mouths. This woman always gives me an orgasmic rush whenever she uses her attitude to make us orgasm in the 69 position.

-=!=-

The Porn Star Belief Machine.

She is wearing an all-in-one crotchless fishnet body stocking and a short leather fashion jacket, with heels, a peaked cap, and a riding crop. I am free to move. I eagerly express my submissive self to my lover as I request her to give me some tactile evidence of her power and love. She uses the knowledge in her mind to firmly drive her desires into me with her own chastising style. As I absorb her energy, I feel my excitement intensify into a pressure cooker of lust and joy. My cock is stiff and sensitively feels every stroke of her whip with maximum pleasure. I want to hold off my orgasm so that the pleasure lasts longer, but she has other ideas and whips me harder and faster. She forcefully and expertly stuns the end of my cock until I can't stop myself from releasing my pulsating, squirting sp*nk. Then I must empty my balls for her complete satisfaction, all over her porn star body, until they throb.

-=!=-

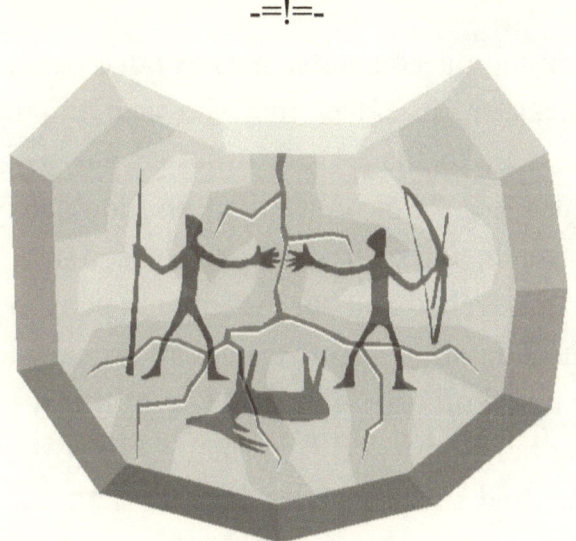

The Demon Dominator Belief Machine.

My fantastic lover's sleek body is bewitching. When she feels like the devil, I become one. I forget to tell her how much I love her while I think about using her as a servile shag piece. She senses and likes that feeling in me. I am captivated by her poetic and alluring body, and I can feel her crafting a spell on my cock with her mind as it swells and stiffens in my clothing. As she notices it grow, she seductively binds my mind to her body with her devilish desires and angelic motion. Within my demonic perception, she has become a tarty temptation of todger tingling talent that wants to be hammered with cock. She slips these ideas into my mind with the ease of a beguiling enchantress while her damp, tingling pussy excites itself on her thoughts. She likes to be taken, and we both know she wants it. I pull her in close, using my cock to caress her pussy, and I unzip her flowing dress. She appears as the goddess of desire in my eye, wearing her yellow lingerie.

As I see the submission collar she has put on in preparation for her pleasure, I realize that she is manipulating my instinctive need to shag. I am full of carnal lust. Now I'm going to use her. "Get on the bed and look sexy!" I say, and she stretches herself submissively across the pillows with her back arched and her legs open. I start to penetrate her with nothing in my mind except an urgency for genital stimulation and orgasm. The first bite of the eye made me hunger for her body, and I can nourish my desires until I have satisfied myself inside her. As I thrust into her, moaning and sighing with masculinity and sweat dripping from my animated, athletic body, I unload my pleasures into her with my swollen cock and grind up against her until she cums. My power is the ability to transform her instinctive feelings from compelling, erotic desire to exhausted, orgasmic relief, and I use overwhelming carnal lust to drive my masculine sexual prowess.

-=!=-

The Fourth Cousin, Twice Removed by Marriage Belief Machine.

My third cousin has grown into a fine young woman, and I always remember enjoying seeing her as a loved and happy little girl. Like any young woman, she has been keen to learn about the advantages nature gave her in the form of a beautiful body. This means that I get the privilege of seeing her investigate herself, if I am quiet when I walk past the guest room at night. I remember the night that she proved to me that she wasn't a child anymore and had started to grow into a woman. It was soon after her eighteenth birthday.

One night I was on my way to bed. As I walked past her bedroom door, a glimpse of movement caught my eye, and I stopped. When I looked in through the open door, I could see and hear the faint movements of a young woman investigating her sex under the sheets. The sight of it fascinated me, and I noticed time seemed to stand still. I don't know how, but I sensed with my intuition that she was fantasizing about being loved too.

The next morning at breakfast, I dropped a comment about being on the landing in the middle of the night, and I asked her if I had woken her up. She put a smile on my face as she replied with the utmost confidence, "No. I wasn't asleep, but I knew you were there." That night, I went to the bathroom three times, and each time I heard her whisper, "Any time you want, I'll be as girlie as shag for you!"

-=!=-

The Domination Deity Belief Machine.

My fantastic lover is one hell of a slut. She's actually a dominatrix who loves to submit to the pleasure of eating her own cum. I discovered her secret desire one night while we were playing in the bedroom. She had tied me up for a teasing session and was sitting on my cock. I suggested that she made me watch while she used her dildo. She climbed off of my stiff, swollen cock, and I looked at her while she took the toy to herself and started to masturbate. It turned me on in my head to know that I had convinced her to do it, because I felt clever. As she pushed the toy in and out, she gently aroused herself by stimulating her clit with her fingers. I knew that she enjoyed controlling me as a submissive, but she wasn't aware that we were controlling each other. "If you tease me more, just show me what else I'm missing," I said. With that, she slid the vibrating toy out of her pussy and brought it up to her mouth. "I bet you'd like to do this." She wavered as she started to lick her own cum off of the toy.

I wanted her to enjoy it more and replied, "You're really turning me on with that thing." As I said it, something clicked inside her head, and she began to smile like a Cheshire cat. Her tongue wiped up the cum on it. I knew I had her in the palm of my hand as I suggestively said, "Now suck the rest of it off of my cock!" She responded by rolling the toy across her breasts and over her body. Then she glided it up my torso to my nipple, where she tickled and teased it gently. With that, she straddled my thighs, lowered her pink and pouting lips to my helmet, and started to worship me.

-=!=-

The Nursey Treatment Belief Machine.

White nurse's jackets with gloves, hats, stockings, and heels. I am sitting in a stirrup chair with safety straps, for genital care. Of my few clinical experiences, having my ball stiffeners replaced is the best. This is probably because the rubber-gloved nursey sisters need to masturbate me so much to get the job done. Mind you, when I think about it, they don't half like issuing pleasure with oral techniques while they're working. I love the feel of the latex on my cock and balls. When they work together, one gives me a nursey blow-job while the other gives me ball-stiffening treatment and professional cock discipline. This is always fantastic, especially when my balls need to be clinically drained. I try to hold off as long as possible before ejaculation, to extend the pleasure.

-=!=-

The Sex Assassin Belief Machine.

My fantastic lover is a beautiful, sexually dominant woman who enjoys extrovert behavior whilst parading herself in kink uniform and bellowing exciting demands for the satisfaction of her lust for sp*nk. She collects all sorts of sex fantasy tricks from her mates and regularly tries them out on me. She often orders me to sit still while she makes me watch her dress up in leather, silk, and latex rubber outfits, which turns me on and makes me hard. I can't help myself from staring at her exquisitely honed body and feeling my cock stiffen. No matter which trick she uses, I always feel pleasure because I love her. One of the best ones happened when she brought home a friend of hers. They took me in turns. One of them took my cock in her mouth while the other kept giving me instructions to sp*nk up. It was as exciting and frustrating as shag. I can still hear it now … "Cum in her mouth!" They were good girls that night. They turned me on and kept me stiff for at least an hour before my lover decided to make me squirt. All it took was one single, maximum-force strike with an extended riding crop on my swollen cock-head. That was enough to instantly force my whole being into an orgasmic mental explosion and a state of exquisite relief and emotional satisfaction.

The Twice the Pleasure Belief Machine.

My fantastic lover and her twin sister enjoy dressing up in fetish gear and working on me as a team, for a laugh. I can't help masturbating over them while they do it. They look so horny while they play with and parade their pussies with attitude and order me to eat their girlie cum as it runs down their rubber stocking–clad thighs. That's when they get excited and use me to rub on their squirting clits. They like taking it in turns to force me up their pussies by straddling my cock and pushing their tits in my mouth. Then they swap round, and one of them squeezes my balls with her shiny black rubber gloves on, while the other gives my cock discipline and correction treatment until it squirts hard under the control of her whip. I get a kick out of watching them wipe my hot sp*nk over each others' tits and licking it off in front of me. I love to shag her sister's massive tits while my lover cleans them, and my cock, with her tongue. It turns them on so much that they involuntarily pussy spray on each others' sexy leather and latex kink uniforms. When they have finished licking up all of my sp*nk, my lover likes to make me lick up all of the pussy spray that they have just squirted over each other from both their stiletto heels and rubber kink uniforms. If I'm lucky, she disciplines my bell-end with her riding crop and constantly orders me to enjoy masturbating myself while her sister licks my balls until I squirt. Then they make me clean both of their shaven pussies as they grind their clits together to improve the access for my tongue.

The Trussed Belief Machine.

My fantastic lover's ego seems to feel seven feet tall to me when I submit to her, as I try to tell her what the beauty and power she possesses does to me. My ability to express myself in words declines as I look into her pale blue eyes and see dazzling crystal irises. They stun me with sexual pleasure, and I get hard thinking about her dominatrix personality. She sees my awkwardness every time I try, and she always encourages me with a loving smile. "Do you want it again?" she says with a compassionate voice. "I enjoy it too!"

My smile turns into a shy grin as I say "Yes please, lover." At these words, she starts to peel off her top and show me her ample, full breasts and tight figure. I strip off my clothes and start to get excited with anticipation as I make my way to the bed. With no bad thoughts in her head, she licks her lips and reaches into the wardrobe for her short-tailed silk lash. She hesitates for a moment because she never quite understands how much I enjoy her athletic ability with that lash. "I think I can do better than this," she says. I reply, "I trust you … What have you got in mind?" "How do you feel about being tied up while you get a blow-job?" she says.

-=!=-

The I'm better than your other lover because: Belief Machine.

She might like to tickle your cock with her tongue, but I like to swallow your sp*nk!

She might shag like a hot date, but I shag like a bitch in heat!

She might wear stockings and heels to look good, but I wear them to shag!

She might lick your cock to please you, but I whip it to excite you!

She might look good dressed up, but I look better naked!

She might know how to sit on top, but I'm gonna ride you like shag!

She might think it's good to wear rubber, but I think it's great for licking cum off of!

She might like to sit on your lap with a smile, but I like to sit on your cock with one!

She might feel good with a damp pussy, but I like a good squirt-emptying!

She might order you to squirt, but I demand you enjoy yourself!

The Love and Beauty Belief Machine.

My fantastic lover is a beautiful woman. My cock goes stiff when she gives me a wink with that knowing smile in her eyes. She often does it when she is brushing her hair in the mirror, just before bedtime. What makes her image more special is that when she does it, I can see her muscle definition in her back and down her spine. As she wriggles her broad hips into the stool, her feminine figure moves gently, like an art form. I always wonder why she licks her lips and blows kisses at the same time she sees my cock under the sheets in the reflection. I think it is because she is as attracted to my sex as I am to her beauty. She always makes love like a good woman, but when she feels sexy, she is the naughtiest girl I know. Last night, she sucked me off like a demented whore and swallowed as much sp*nk as I could give her. And if it is true that love is a feeling, I can guarantee that that I still love her after a sixteen-year relationship. It's not my heart that aches … it's my balls.

-=!=-

The Teasing the Talent Belief Machine.

My fantastic lover leaned over to me last night while I was watching television and said, "I'm wet!" I smiled and turned to her with a sparkle in my eye. Shortly after-wards, I got my own back on her and gently whispered into her ear, "I'm hard!" She grinned. These exchanges went on all night, and both of us knew that she was going to get shagged good and hard when we went to bed.

-=!=-

The Ultimate Love Bitch Belief Machine.

My fantastic lover whispered in my ear the other night, "I can't cum on any other man … I've always been stuck on you." I replied, "Can you bitch me up with banter so high that I never want to come down?"

-=!=-

Who said these other phrases for one or the other of the genders?

I'm your little sp*nk slut.

I like bending over with my pussy out.

I'm gonna push my tits in your mouth while I shag you.

I'm gonna teach you to get off in my pussy.

I'm gonna shag you until your balls are aching with emptiness.

I'm gonna slap you around with my pussy so hard that you'll need nursey treatment.

I feel like emptying my pussy and forcing you to lick up my cum out of a dog bowl.

I'm gonna sit on your cock and tell you off for not sp*nking.

You like it when I order you to give me your sp*nk, don't you?

That's nice enough to sit on, that is.

Me and my beauty queen mates are going to be girlie as shag on your cock.

I need your shag, sir.

You're in love with me cos I got a pussy, aren't you?

I'm gonna make you clean my pussy with your tongue all night cos I like it!

While I'm making you eat my cum, I'm gonna make you squirt so hard you're gonna feel faint.

Darling, that shag we had last night would have killed a normal man!

Come here, you. I wanna stick my nose up your pussy.

Get your pussy out, sexy. Sugar Daddy wants one!

A proper shag involves spraying sweat and cum everywhere.

I know you like my personality because I've got a massive cock.

Now that I know how submissive you are, I'm gonna ride you like shag.

Tell me how much you like my cock.

Sex should be a sport for people who love each other.

Both me and my cock are in love with you.

You look like a million-dollar shag.

I am first officer on a vessel commanded by God!

I'm gonna stuff your pussy so full of cock that you're gonna gag on my sp*nk!

My lover must be a shagged-up lesbian because she loves cock.

Last night, I knocked loads of lesbian fantasies out of my lover's head with my cock.

My cock is so much bigger than average that it is classified as a lesbian straightener.

If I invite you to my house for a shag, will you do the washing up?

There is no status in society better than "friend and lover".

You need a good pussy shagging, you do!

"No ladies' toy should ever be bigger than my cock!"

You deserve to be filled up with my sp*nk.

Get up my pussy, you shag!

Of course we can pleasure ourselves by sharing my body.

"I'm ordering you to be a flirtatious girlie, tart." "I've just cum, Sugar Daddy!"

The idea of your pussy slides through my brain like a pair of cum-soaked, silk knickers.

I got me some Bodashus Ta Ta.

Do you want to make this permanent?

-=!=-

Solutions

The Sandstorm Belief Machine.

My fantastic lover is a brilliant dancer. When I see her body move and pose, I must worship her female form for the pleasure of knowing that she feels admired. To see her graceful silhouette slide into view against the ambient rainbow of a morning sunrise is to welcome love into your life every day. Her face is natural artwork from her first tear to her latest smile, and when her body moves, she becomes poetry to the eye. She has an amazing effect on me when she struts her stuff. The first time she danced for me, I realized how impressive she was and nearly popped with pleasure. When the curtains went back on the stage, I felt her body draw my attention instantly, and I couldn't be diverted from enjoying the sight of her movement. I couldn't believe my eyes when I saw the confidence with which she darted her sexy form to and fro with fiery, energetic motion. She moved with a presence that was in time with a sandstorm of amplified, rhythmic sound. Her enjoyment and expression were fantastic to ogle, and when she strutted her ample torso, she looked so proud with her marvelous poise. It made me shine with pleasure to see her foxy female body flitting and flirting about. As she changed her routine from good to better to best, I realized that I was witnessing the gift of a sex goddess.

-=!=-

The Sacred Fantasy Belief Machine.

My fantastic lover often gets an insistent urge to force my sp*nk out of the end of my massive cock. This sort of cock manipulation can only be learned by a woman who enjoys the act of loving and pleasuring her man. With her willful mind, she intelligently uses her confident, beauty queen attitude to take pleasure in extrovertly displaying herself. The liquid rainbow suit generates pleasurable responses in my mind as she seductively writhes about, making herself cum. Her perfect physique smoothly slides around, generating sexual signals in the form of desire, excitement, and anticipation. I can't help but drift into a trance as I worship her immaculate female form writhing in my mind. I feel a sense of overpowering admiration and awe for her beauty as my cock gets swollen and stiff. She gives me total forgiveness for my lust as she straddle-shags me and drives her orgasm down onto my manhood. I love it when she encourages me to sp*nk by offering up her beautiful breasts to my mouth.

A Night on the Sp*nk Farm Belief Machine.

My fantastic lover is so horny that I can very rarely hold off orgasm until she is satisfied. We have discussed this phenomenon many times and found various solutions to the problem. The best one was to change our priorities from orgasm to pleasure generation by shagging. We found this out a while back when we went on a trip for a weekend last year. After we left, I found and read the booking ticket. It was for a place in the next county called Hollow Acres, and it was some form of recreational retreat on farmland for naughty lesbians. I was a little confused as to why we were going to be accepted in such a place, but my lover suggested that this was actually a business trip, and if it was a good concern, she would buy and manage the farm. When we arrived on that Saturday afternoon, we were shown to a room with lots of cupboard space and a four-poster bed. I decided to wait in the room and listen to music whilst my lover was taken on a tour of the complex by the current owner. I fell asleep and dreamed.

Dreaming Of		
Who	Doing	With
Maid	Cleaning Rooms	Feather Duster
Cha Lady	Tea Break	Sugar Sprinkler
Window Cleaner	Cleaning Windows	Rubber Gloves andHot Water
Odd Jobber	Electrical Safety Check	Two Volt Pencil Battery and a Lamp
Burglar	Take It All	Swag Bag

By the time my lover came back, I had learned just how far the staff were prepared to take their service, and I looked forward to buying the hotel with my future wife. She said that the concept of lesbianism had been bothering her all day, and she felt rather naughty herself. She asked me if I could straighten her head out with my cock. As she straddled me on the bed, I told her that I would love to take care of her, but I was a bit tired and probably wouldn't be able to sp*nk up. Without hesitation she immediately replied, "It looks like everybody's being naughty today!" "Yes," I said. "Even the staff." "No," she said. "They were the customers!"

-=!=-

The Welcome to Marriage-Dom Belief Machine.

I want to 'spouse' you. If you don't marry me … you're shagged!

-=!=-

The Madam's Wedding Ceremony Belief Machine.

My next wife controls the fantastic lust that makes me desire my other submissive partners like a professional madam. If I had my way, the ribs on my condom would represent our individual wedding bands. As she orders me to shag all of them one by one, I can feel the tight, elasticated, latex rubber clinging to my swollen cock while I excite their pussies. After I have finished pleasuring them to orgasm, my madam lover rubs her stockings over it until it is dry, polished, and shiny. I peel off the empty rubber sheath, and she climbs over my supine body, commanding the other naughty little sluts to join in. Then they start to stimulate my mind with their sexy fantasies and erotic thoughts going directly into my brain. Our unified pleasure in sex is excited as my madam lover forces her wet, soft pussy into my open mouth and constantly tickles my cock and balls into a feathery orgasm of squirting sp*nk. With a massive sigh of relief, we are all finally married.

(For a list of the things that my naughty little sluts said, see the following fantasies: Coffee and Biscuits, Bitchy Banter, Audible Rainbow, and Yes, Miss Madam, in that order.)

The Sex Maniac's Kiss Belief Machine.

My fantastic wife is keen to compete with all the ghosts of the past and win. She has my full support and regularly practices the arts of the professional female, specifically to improve our shagging experiences. Now that we've been together for some time, I feel comfortable enough to relax in front of her as she communicates exciting fantasies to me whilst making me orgasm. I feel like the ultimate self when she submits to her porn star feelings as I shag her, and she experiences my masculinity in the submissive way. I want her to be a lover who shags like a goddess and can rescue me from my obsessive pleasure addiction with her love. If the devil sends distractions in the middle of the night, my lover knows how to make me feel as though I don't need them, because she can shag like an angel. A simple pleasure ritual that symbolizes the happiness we find in each other should do the job. A perfect French kiss, for example. I want to feel that there will never be a woman who can equal her spirit and determination at keeping our relationship together.

-=!=-

The Power Experiment Belief Machine.

While I was at work yesterday, I couldn't help thinking about sex all day. I walked in the door after making my way home, and my wife greeted me as she saw my face. I had no idea how, but the glint that flashed in her eye told me that she knew what was in my mind—and that she wanted to cooperate. Without hesitation and with a previously unknown confidence, I started the conversation boldly.

He: "By the time I've finished with you, you're gonna be so shagged that you won't be able to walk tomorrow, and you won't mind lying in bed all day thinking about it!"

She: "My God! Your balls are massive!"

I threw my briefcase to the floor, and as it landed, the lid burst open and all the paperwork scattered over the carpet. I didn't care!

She: "My God! I've just cum!"

I looked at her with a powerful glare as I ripped open my shirt and provocatively twitched my chest muscles in her direction. She stared at my ribcage as I expanded it to impress her.

She: "My God! Chase me! Chase me!"

She turned and ran with the speed of a doe rabbit, and like a mad march hare, I bound up the stairs after her. As she ran up the stairs, I could hear her teasing me and driving me forward.

She "My God! I want your sp*nk!"

Before either of us had finished running around the bedroom with athletic prowess, we had both escaped our clothes with more mystery than a Houdini magic trick.

He: "Get on the bed and look sexy!"

She submitted to my command instantly and stretched her body to full length with a hopeful look on her face.

She: "My God! Sir, I'm yours. What would you like to do to me?"

He: "You're my bitch! And you're gonna be a happy one!"

She squealed with excitement and responded to me by opening her legs. By now my cock was as hard as iron and tingling with pleasure. The sight of her pussy urged me to climb onto her svelte body. She moaned with a purr while I started to penetrate her.

He: "Say it, bitch!"

She: "My God! Take me! Take me, you handsome bastard!"

The power rushed through my veins as I forced my cock into her vagina. This woman knew I was her better half, the powerful half of her "love and power" life system. I was enjoying her.

She: "My God! I love you! Give it to me! I want more! I want it all!"

He: "Take this, then, you beautiful bitch!"

With the confidence of a true male, I thrust my cock farther and faster into to her as sweat and testosterone poured out of my body. I unloaded my masculine balls deep into her pussy with a pulsating, squirting orgasm that could kill a normal man. I had finally achieved the status of sex god, and she loved it.

The Happily Ever After Belief Machine.

And they all lived happily ever after!

The End

-=!=-

The Final Clue (Dinosaur for Breakfast.)

My wife and I went out for a walk before breakfast with a couple of her friends. As we were walking along the ridge side path, along the top of the cliff, I couldn't help noticing a huge dinosaur lazily wandering around below us. I stopped and assessed the ground contours in the valley below, and I realized that the sand near the shore was shining. As I realized what this indicated, the dinosaur looked up at me. It paused for a moment as it surveyed the potential for danger; we had just entered its field of view. I turned and said to her and her friends, "You wedge this lever under that rock and place a pivot underneath it. When the dinosaur gets to the right place, pull the lever!" She and her friends looked a bit bemused for a short while as they whispered amongst themselves and then carried out the preparations. I walked away smiling and disappeared behind a tree. After a while, the dinosaur walked into exactly the right position, called ground zero, and my wife pulled the lever. "Great Shot!" I exclaimed, as I came out from behind a different tree. The dinosaur was dead! Then my wife asked me in a very curious manner, "What is it that you do for your job?" With a winning smile on my face, I casually replied, "Didn't I say before? I kill rock-hard dinosaurs." For some reason, that's when all their loin cloths coincidentally fell off, full of cum!.

Comments, a Song, Poems, and a Joke

It must have been obvious to you by now that this book is designed to introduce a style of thinking about sexual activity which encourages your partners to think about sex in a manner that makes them smile when they look at you. If you have chosen to be a sex god or sex goddess, then you may appreciate the following advice to guide you in how to approach the task.

1. Remember the idea is to get the best package deal you can, in a partner. This includes the assets of looks, personality, lifestyle, bank account, employment, property, personal standards, and friendship circle.

2. Looks are listed first because it is the most important asset. The others can all come third place to the size of the bank account.

3. All men should wear a suit for social occasions, and all women should wear stockings and heels in bed.

4. It doesn't matter what nine belief machines a sex deity partner learns, as long as it's the nine you want and he or she is excellent at oral sex.

5. Remember that training your partner to exaggerate about how fantastically brilliant you are in bed will help boost your ego like a NASA lift-off.

6. If your partners scream, "Oh, God! I can't stop cumming!" you can only stay in orbit as long as you can hear them and they are not stuffing their heads under the pillows to prevent upsetting the neighbors.

Song: Woke Up This Mornin'

Woke up this mornin' upside-down in my bed.

Pricked up one ear, not a sound in my head.

I opened one eye to see the new day.

I stared at the mirror and heard myself say,

The CHORUS

What the hell did I do? What occurred last night?

Did I get run over, or was there was a fight?

I feel really awful, so ghastly and foul.

Head throbbing so much, makes me want to howl.

Well, my head felt heavy, my muscles felt meek.

I felt kinda sick, and my stomach felt weak.

My brain felt dizzy, and my skin had lost its glow.

How many did I drink last night? I don't really know.

Repeat CHORUS

Then a voice spoke out from under the sheet.

A dry croaky throat that started to bleat,

"Welcome to marriage. I'm your new wife.

We'll be together for the rest of your life."

Repeat CHORUS

Those words hit my ears like a hammer to ice.

I wanted to know if she looked really nice.

I turned my head round so that I could see.

With God as my witness, she looked worse than me.

Repeat CHORUS

She had one dodgy eye and pale, wonky lips.

She weighed three hundred pounds,
I couldn't see her hips.

She had broken teeth and a half-bent ear.

I gulped and I smiled, then felt like turning queer.

Repeat CHORUS

Well, I phoned up my lawyer and I asked for a divorce.

He said, "Yes, I can do it, but I want cash, of course.

If you think I come cheap, you're havin' a laugh.

So count all your assets, cos she will want half."

Repeat CHORUS

I said straight to her face, "The vows are for breakin'.

I'm throwing you out. Don't care what your takin'."

Well, it wasn't very much when I tallied my money,

But the less that I had made it seem more funny.

Repeat CHORUS

Well, the lessons of life are much clearer today.

I need quality women that I think should stay.

So when you're out drinking, try not to look big.

Never challenge your mates to play "Pull-a-pig".

-=!=-

Poem: A Wise Head on Young Shoulders

A sex robot that feels is what I be,
But a robot that's broken is all they see.
All I need is a mind that's free;
Then I'll be happy for me, me, me.

-=!=-

Young and eager, with soul of fire.
Mechanical skeleton, nerves of wire.
Soldier of fortune for your hire.
I burn my bridges to fuel the pyre.

-=!=-

I fight like mad, but never kill.
A mind of steel and iron will.
Use pen, not sword, and mental skill.
Winning the game through disciplined drill.

-=!=-

I'm so young and strong, I cannot lose.
The world's full of things for me to use.
Not gonna drive; I'm gonna power cruise.
Gonna steer through time on a course I choose.

-=!=-

My suit looks good when I am nude.

My silver bullet is my attitude.
I'm sex on legs, a handsome dude.
A very bit horny and amusingly rude.

-=!=-

Effort means nothing ... success is the game.
I have ambition without any shame.
Gonna fight my way to fortune and fame
With power and love, and a heart of flame.

-=!=-

Brace yourself; I'm coming through
Like the first steam engine when it was new.
Gonna change the world with what I do.
When I land, you'll know how fast I flew.

-=!=-

Gonna take on the world from day to day.
Gonna live all my dreams, treat life as play.
Gonna burn myself out, not fade away.
Gonna chase white tigers, and dragon slay.

-=!=-

Poem: Marry Me Properly

Hello, my dear. I'm looking for a wife,
A lovely young lady who wants a nice life.
How would you be my trouble and strife?
Would you do it properly?

Would you do the laundry in the nude?
Can I pinch your bum like a handsome dude?
If I licked your tit, would I get sued?
Would you do it properly?

Would you wear your heels in bed, my dear?
What about swinging off the chandelier?
Will you shag me straight if I turn queer?
Would you do it properly?

If I stub my toe, will you suck my dick?
Give me nursey treatment till I feel sick?
Bring home two mates and let me pick?
Would you do it properly?

Will you wear no knickers when we go out?
When I look at you, will you tease and pout?
When I make you cum, will you scream and shout?
Would you do it properly?

Will you wear stockings and miniskirts?
Wear peephole bras and see-through shirts?
Use a riding crop, but stop when it hurts?
Would you do it properly?

Will you let me love your tits, so round,
And be your obsessed pussy hound?
Can I nuzzle my nose in your sweet mound?
Would you do it properly?

Will you let me shave your pubic hair?
When you see my cock, be impressed and stare?
Will you act like a doggy with your a*se in the air?
Would you do it properly?

You can be dom and I can be sub.
Kiss me in the shower and shag me in the tub!
You can ride like hell till you're in the club!
Would you do it properly?

Will you treat me like a toy in bed at night?
When I ask for sex, always get it right!
Never say no or give me a fright!
Would you do it properly?

Will you open your legs when I want a bunk?
Make me feel like a man and not a young punk!
Will you turn me on by eating my sp*nk?
Would you do it properly?

Will you let me shag your tits
And use a dildo on your clit
While you're wearing bondage kit?
Would you do it properly?

Will you want your pussy to get a spank
When I catch you playing a prank,
Then wind me up by asking me to wank?
Would you do it properly?

If you do it for free and don't charge rent,
I will think that you are heaven sent!
I'll love you like the devil and never repent!
Would you do it properly?

Will you be a sex assassin? That's no joke!
Be a woman with a pussy that needs a good poke!
A fantastic whore that breaks normal blokes!
Would you do it properly?

I'm superhuman when in bed,
And I'm a mad shagger; let it be said,
A sex robot love machine you're going to wed!
Cos I can do it properly!

-=!=-

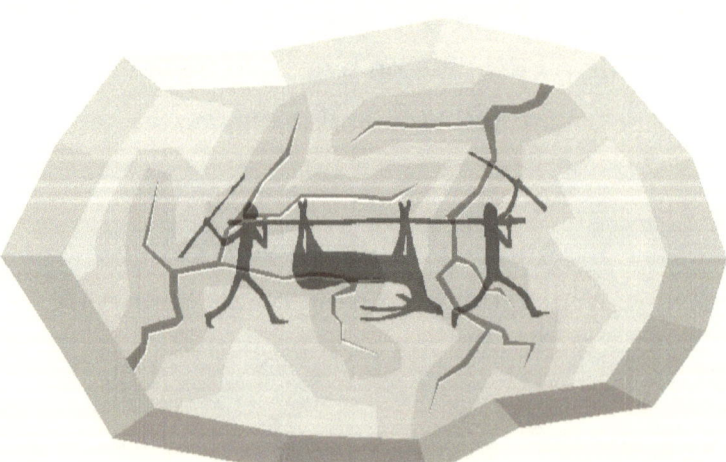

A Shagging Stupid Joke

If you were the manager of a rubber dolly manufacturer, the most genius thing I can recommend is to have the word "stupid" printed on the product in a convenient place. This would allow a fascinating phenomenon in the sales department that could enable the advertising team to state that if a customer wants to be shagging stupid, this will be the best product on the market. Consequently, people in future years will be walking in to sex shops all over the country just for the fun of saying things like, "If I pay you shed loads of money, will I be shagging stupid after I leave the shop?"

The shopkeeper would also be within his rights to say, "If you can accept our no-returns policy, I would be shagging stupid not to let you."

In order to mimic these brave people, who are not afraid of ridicule, if you and your partner were to paint the words "I am stupid" on each others' foreheads, and then have sex with each other, would you both be shagging stupid? If you flipped her over into the doggy position and stuck it up her a*se, do you think she would have written on her back, "You're in the wrong hole … Are you really that shagging stupid?" If you really wanted to go for it, you could say to your wife, "Now I'm going to shag you stupid!" and she would probably reply, "Well, at least you know my name … Which proves you're not that shagging stupid after all!" At the point when you remember that this is your wife and not your mistress, you will then be able to say, "Of course I know your name … Which proves I'm not that shagging stupid, actually!" And just to wind you up for a laugh, your wife can say, "Are you doing this while you are thinking of your mistress? Because that would be very shagging stupid indeed." If you were to reply to this question, "No, dear. I was thinking that rather than impersonating a rubber doll, you should buy me a proper one because its tits are bigger than yours," that would be extremely shagging stupid.

If you married your wife for the right reasons, she will take you at your word and go to the sex shop to get a rubber dolly, because she has found out that you like being shagging stupid for fun. When you get home the next night, she will inform you that she has brought home a mate who is so shagging stupid that she hasn't realized that she is here to be shagged stupid as part of a threesome. She tells you that to get the best blow-job you've ever had, all you have to do is touch her breasts with your left hand. As you rush into the bedroom with your cock out in your right hand, you see the rubber dolly on the bed with white lingerie on. From behind your location, your wife then exclaims, "I bet you know how to feel shagging stupid now, don't you?" At this point, you will learn whether you have got the bottle to be shagging stupid for a laugh. Your wife knew when she bought the rubber dolly that the only way you could prove your character is to shag the rubber dolly stupid while she lays on the bed, playing with herself for your entertainment. This is because rubber dollies just aren't as good as women, and that would be shagging stupid to believe. My best guess at what you should do at this point in your life is to suggest to your wife that you want the blow-job from her, because no other woman or representation thereof will do. That way, neither of you will ever end up being shagging stupid!

However, if you wanted to double-bluff your wife into believing that you are braver than she expected, another option might be to go through with being shagging stupid and shagging the rubber dolly stupid. At this point, she might actually be surprised at you for breaking the situation with humor. Your wife may sarcastically ask you whether or not she could have improved the experience. If she does, try suggesting that next time there should be a repetitive riff playing on the stereo that repeats the phrase, "I want your sperm!" This way you will have a constant reminder of your wife while you were trying to ejaculate. If you think about it, that isn't actually shagging stupid!

The last comment that comes to mind is that bearing in mind the number of rubber dolly sales that are instigated through practical jokes, it appears that it is quite normal to be shagging stupid. Given this fact, because we all seek social acceptance in some form or other, and there is a social stigma about rubber dollies, it is shagging stupid not to be shagging stupid in the first place. Now, is that shagging stupid or what? Consequently, the best and funniest way to prove you are quite normal compared to all those people who resent spending their entire weekly wage on living expenses seems to be to walk into your nearest outlet for rubber dollies and loudly say, "I want to be shagging stupid. How much money do you want?" If the shopkeeper is not shagging stupid, he will guide you to the top shelf, where you will see the latest line of luxury model rubber dollies, which have words like "mad" or "insane" printed on the packet. The rubber dolly manufacturer must have done some more thinking about his advertising campaign, because the sign on the middle shelf says, "Don't be shagging stupid … For three times the price, you can be shagging insane!"

-=!=-

Love Mania Philosophy

This club is designed for people who practice the art of producing pleasure in the minds of other club members, using personalized sexual fantasies. Before using a fantasy for this purpose, it would be wise to understand the mutually agreed philosophy of club members.

I think; therefore I am.

I exist as a living intelligence inside a thought-operated, biochemical machine.

I am an animal called man.

We are social animals because this
is the intelligent choice.

We share pleasure to enhance our existence.

The nature of existence is existence and time.

Time is the most valuable asset we have.

We seek to share time in positive
emotional states of mind.

Our communication medium is heterosexual fantasies.

These exchanges give us pleasure, excitement, and joy.

We associate the joy we experience with
our fantasy partner's personality.

We enjoy each other as people.

Within the human mind, we exist as "positive vital entities". Some people use the word *soul* to describe what we call the conscious spirit. The consciousness is deemed to be the representation of the personality or character of an individual human being:

To communicate these fantasies is to generate
pleasure in the mind of another, with permission.

They are designed to cause pleasant
effects in the imagination.

We learn to associate this pleasure
with our partner's identity.

Pleasure on contact with these
partners develops over time.

With this development, we can exist
with a shared love of life.

We aim to share familiarity, acceptance, and
pleasure on contact with our partners.

Those with whom we achieve this knowledge
will be deemed our life partners.

The more successful relationships within the team have been developed over time with dedication and loyalty as the main priority. All have been developed with the objective of falling in love - and most importantly, with honest communication between partners. With the fail-safe standard of friendship set into the relationships at the beginning, all of them have been a success to some degree or other.

Friendship first. Love always.

-=!=-

Rainbow

The rainbow emotional generation idea system works on belief. The principal of how it works is that color is enjoyable to perceive, and that we can train our responses with belief and practice. After some practice with this system, we found that we could generate some psychological reactions by wearing clothing of specific colors. This clothing served as a psychological tool, and we each became aware of its potential in ourselves and each other for the generation of emotional effects. The colors we used were as follows.

Transparent Crystal	to represent	Purity
Brilliant White	to represent	Love
Passionate Pink	to represent	Rapture
Pillar Box Red	to represent	Pleasure
Flame Orange	to represent	Passion
Bright Yellow	to represent	Desire
Luxury Green	to represent	Gratitude
Electric Blue	to represent	Energy
Royal Purple	to represent	Joy
Jet Black	to represent	Power

The rainbow system comes in five levels.

Novice

This system is for training novice extroverts, and it helps them gain experience of the responses that are available from their partners. Best used with a dance regime. A novice wears one color at a time and learns one sex lover's belief machine. This level is for learning to entertain her partner. The main priority is to pick a dance that you both like.

Intermediate

This system is for training experienced extroverts, and it helps them develop their desired personal, emotional response repertoire with their partners. Best used with an experienced fantasy. An intermediate wears three colors at a time and practices her three favorite sex lover's belief machines. The main priority in this situation is familiarity with communication.

Qualified

A qualified wears five colors at a time and practices her five favorite sex lover's belief machines. This level is for learning how to produce the correct emotion in your partner. The main priority in this situation is honesty.

Expert

This system is for advanced extroverts and is a full emotion generation system that relies on life force energy radiation through color filters in order to operate. Best used with the presentation of a sexual gift fantasy. An expert wears seven colors at a time and practices her seven favorite sex lover's belief machines. This level is for learning to switch between the desired responses in her partner while designing your gift.

Deity

Female Sex Goddess—Diva. The core principle of the Fluid Rainbow Liquid Crystal Energy System is that we exist as positive, vital entities. Our radiated thoughts and feelings may be detected by others and responded to. With experience in the rainbow system, it is possible to learn how to exchange positive feelings and enjoy doing it by transmitting and receiving visual messages. The images sent represent beauty and arousal, and the rewards gained are confidence and pleasure. A deity wears nine colors at a time and practices her nine favorite sex lover's belief machines. This level is for learning to deliver more powerful performance for a higher impact fantasy. The dance leads on to a sex lover's belief machine that is of your joint design and will be her gift.

Male Sex God—Master. The core principals of the Fluid Flame Liquid Crystal Energy System are the intent of developing mutual love and respect using the methods of cooperation and kindness, through the medium of trust by consistently generating the response of pleasure. An experienced system user can confidently project powerful signals and cause in others the response of respect and pleasure.

The result of learning to use the rainbow system properly is to understand the pleasure to be had in perceiving color. From fire-work displays to brightly dressed people, the results are the same: "I see; therefore I feel."

Some Other Concepts Examined

Concept (Available for the use of)

The Positive Vital Entity Belief System is an example of a lifestyle concept that is designed upon the pursuit of pleasure. This component-based system is represented as a case study. This helps other people strip down and examine their own lifestyles, and it helps them identify their personal preferences of lifestyle components and prioritize them into a practical system.

Lifestyle

This is defined as the way in which a person lives. Because style is a way of doing something, it is reasonable to consider lifestyle as a method of survival. We need a good one!

Feelings

If you see that a feeling is a detectable state of mind that can be defined as an emotional generator, it is possible to classify feelings as positive, neutral, or negative. When you try to measure these feelings, you can compare them by the level of impression that they make in the mind. By understanding your best feelings, you can generate them at will with the belief machines.

Happiness

This can be defined as a mental state which generates a belief and is driven or enabled by a positive feeling. No matter what activity or thought that generates the feeling, this feeling can always be described as pleasure. Pleasure makes us happy!

Satisfaction

In the event that a positive mental state is experienced for a long enough duration, it will become normality and appear normal by comparison to other feelings or states of mind. If you have no requirement to act upon or change your current mental state, this can be deemed satisfactory.

Religion

There are several ways to define and understand the word *religion*. The dictionary describes the word as meaning "a belief in, and worship of, a god or gods".

Spirituality

The word *spirit* and all its suffixes have a total of twelve definitions between them. "A person's character and feelings" is the first and main usage.

The Sex Lover's Fantasy Mind-Driver System: Conclusions

This book was an attempt to encourage experimentation, using sexual fantasies as a medium, to promote happiness within a relationship and a better understanding of the sexual expectations each of us have. With varying degrees of success throughout the research team, we learned the following things.

Love is not sexual.

Sex is not love.

This mind-driver system can be used as a sexual method of generating pleasure and love.*

Our personality combined with our knowledge dictates our sexual style and choices.#

*Note: This works by associating the pleasure we feel for our partners with their identities and personalities. Although there are many definitions of love, the simple one we derived from and for this system is, "I take pleasure in your existence."

#Note: The phrase we use to describe this point is, "The personality drives the machine," where the machine is our physical brain and all of its' information, beliefs and responses, and the personality is that which makes decisions intelligently.

We also discovered that the best and suggested manner in which to consider the material in this book should be to treat it as a fantasy testing system, with examples.

Consequently:

> *A personality can apply a concept within the framework of a fantasy character, using a designed sexual fantasy that is agreed by both parties, for the purposes of generating pleasure within a relationship.*
>
> *The purpose of such a sex game is to enhance the ability and encourage the willingness of the members of the relationship to enjoy contact time with each other.*
>
> *If the members of the relationship manage their part of it and value the feelings of their partners, the couple can develop and achieve a friendly, loving association with each other as human beings.*

A Personal Observation: Further Considerations for Readers

A scientist, theorist, or logic expert can reasonably deduce that the concepts of religion and spirituality promote social behavior within a person, and each of them is perceived from a different perspective.

Religion appears to be perceived from the perspective of an individual who chooses to conform to a group theory in order to gain social acceptance.

We all appreciate social acceptance. This is why we had to get our partners' agreement to any of the ideas that we experimented with, to prevent the possible bad feeling generated by rejection. In the same way that common ideas within the relationship were used, social acceptance can be gained within a group by the use of generic ideas and beliefs that are common to the group. This helps us associate with each other and prevents stigma.

Spirituality appears to be based on the principal of internal satisfaction in order to promote the self. This should reduce the group workload for survival purposes by creating people with fewer problems.

The concept of self-improvement is natural and possibly instinctive, and it does not become greed until the accumulation principle is over used to the dissatisfaction of others. Bearing this in mind, jealousy in other people can be avoided within a group by using the sharing principle. In this book, we are learning pleasure-craft systems, and we can be perceived as better people if all the group members actively enjoy participating and generating pleasure for everyone concerned. To consider this practice as a skill is advantageous.

With the exception that both of these personal life systems expect you to believe in life after death, and that there is no physical proof of a godhead, the concepts of religion and spirituality appear to be designed to promote contentment and good feelings within an individual. The purpose of both of these concepts appears to aid social conduct within a group. This promotes behavioral conduct and assists the group to coexist socially in a physical environment.

Given that time is a person's most valuable asset, and that each of us wishes to spend as many happy days on the planet as possible, it is reasonable to conclude that we need an efficient balance of varied activity to create a satisfactory lifestyle.

The pursuit of happiness is our ambition, and we hope to enjoy doing it. However, in order to live a functional lifestyle, we must seek a practical state of mind with which to operate within society. This involves only generating positive states of mind in a way that is socially acceptable and at a convenient time.

The Positive Vital Entity Belief System lifestyle concept involves generating personal pleasure for the satisfaction of the self and others. We do this with the requirement of social acceptance within our local group, in order to reduce the amount of interference from others and therefore reduce the average amount of problems that the local community needs to handle should we offend anybody by accident.

If you understand the concepts and associated belief systems of the self and the group, you can be a cooperating individual and get along fine in your relationships. This logical conclusion does not dictate total acceptance of all in your society. It allows for toleration of others and reasonable communication potential when a problem occurs.

The ceremonies and rituals surrounding this suggested lifestyle allow people to develop life systems that are designed to promote social conduct within groups.

This indicates that the human spirit is associated with an individual perception of life, and also the desire to generate good feelings within ourselves and other people, for the benefit of each other.

I conclude that the intent to act intelligently involves generating positive feelings within your local group and not taking advantage of those who respond kindly. You do not need to understand whether or not a "God" exists in order to do this. Therefore, "God" need not exist as anything other than an abstract concept and could be defined as the spirit of man on a good day. Religion and spirituality are not necessary because they are a personal choice, but humanity involves all of us!

-=!=-

The Below Competition
Actually Exists

In order to win this competition, you must present and donate a manuscript for a radio-style broadcast. The broadcast will last no longer than five minutes, and the manuscript will contain less than one thousand and one (1,001) words from an English dictionary.

The purpose of this competition is to allow the public to enter a fantasy that may be considered for a future book.

-=!=-

In order to enter the competition, all you need to do is commit to the following eighteen instructions. Please abide by them accurately.

1. Invent a descriptive name for your fictional character in less than six words.

2. Using the example profiles in this sex engineering project book as a guide, answer the following questions about your fictional characters' profile.

- What is their descriptive name?

- What is their style of heterosexual behavior?

- What phrase describes their personal perspective on life?

- Which type or class of image do they try to present?

- What motivates them to perform well?

- What is their lifelong ambition?

- What is their current goal?

- What would be their ideal vocation?

- What is the best thing they have ever done?

- Which sex lover's gift did they design?

- What is their favorite catchphrase?

- What subjects are they best qualified to comment on?

- What is their voice type?

3. Explain why the world should know about this fictional character in no more than forty words.

4. Express this fictional character's gift as a sex lover's belief machine using no more than eight hundred words.

5. The title of the sex lover's belief machine will be:

   "A Bold Birthday Surprise!"

6. The fictional character will be using, as a tool, "The Personal Definition of Love" that you constructed as a concept with your partner earlier in this book. The theme

will be accurately reflected by the descriptive name of the fictional character.

7.   All entries will be copyrighted in the actual name of the author of the entry.

8.   The name and e-mail address of the author will be detailed.

9.   The following statement will be expressed in print within the document:

> "The Rock Hard Dinosaur Killer will own the copyright and royalties for this creation, upon entry to the competition."

10. Record your work in a .docx document, entitled:

> "Sexual-Belief-Machine-Competition-Entry.docx".

11. A person may enter the competition as many times as he or she wishes.

12. Each entry will be considered as a separate entry.

13. All competition entries will be in the form of an A5 document (with no more than 6 sides of size 14 text, without images) using the .docx file type, to be ready for judging.

14. No communication will be entered into between the Rock Hard Dinosaur Killer and the author of the copyrighted competition entry.

15. All entries to the competition that are deemed to be valid and legal will be entered into the relevant database, or other mind-driver system.

> Note: if the concepts of destruction or harm are expressed in a fantasy creation, that entry will be deemed invalid!

> Note: every word in the author's creation must have been defined as a word in the English language, with the use of a dictionary.

16. The competition entries will be judged by comparison to each other.

17. The e-mail address will be accessible by my local police force.

18. Send one rhetorical e-mail with one competition entry as an email attachment to:

> dinosaur.killer.competition@gmail.com.

-=!=-

Next Step After Entering the Competition:

Wait for the Publication *A Bold Birthday Surprise*©.
The proposed book will contain the top 104
winning entries from the competition.

-=!=-

Note:

Although condoms are useful tools, the subject of personal contraception methods should be investigated with the guidance of a professional sex adviser.

-=!=-

This is a Sex Fantasy Engineering Project, which employs a general-purpose, relationship system–enhancement tool.

What is it?	**What can you do with it?**
Technical erotica	Have fun
Concept manual for sex technicians	Learn sexual ideas
Database of sex fantasies	Discover relationships
Blue art	Feel good

How do you use it?

Learn to communicate with your
partners using the simple rules

Understand the concepts and how they turn you on
Exchange the erotica with your partners
for the purpose of pleasure

Build new and exciting sex fantasies

What can you get out of it?

Realize pleasure as a mental art form
Generate loving relationships

Jointly improve your sex life with your partners

-=!=-